About the Author

Sujit is currently the head of institutional equities for HSBC, India. He has over twenty-five years of experience in the financial markets doing macro, strategy, sector and company research as well as investing globally across asset classes. Sujit completed his MBA from the S P Jain Institute of Management & Research in Mumbai in 1993 and has spent most of his working career based in Singapore, having recently returned to India. During his research days, Sujit was consistently ranked as a top three analyst globally, and in Asia by Asiamoney and Institutional Investor. Among various financial institutions, Sujit has spent close to a decade with firms like UBS and also ran his own global macro, multi-strategy hedge fund from Singapore for a few years.

A Wall Street View of Rural India

Sujit Sahgal

A Wall Street View of Rural India

Olympia Publishers
London

www.olympiapublishers.com
OLYMPIA PAPERBACK EDITION

A CIP catalogue record for this title is
available from the British Library.

ISBN: 978-1-78830-598-3

First Published in 2020

Olympia Publishers
Tallis House
2 Tallis Street
London
EC4Y 0AB
Printed in Great Britain

Acknowledgements

First and foremost, I want to sincerely thank Veena, my wife, who has given me the confidence and self-belief to take up this writing project. She has put up with my long-drawn effort on innumerable weekends when I sacked up at home writing. Not to mention tolerate the constant and understandably irritating sound of keyboard tapping while she tried to catch some sleep! Her inputs on the title and cover went a long way in helping me make up my mind.

I would like to thank Mr Pradeep Kashyap, founder of Mart Rural — a rural marketing consultancy. I had taken the help of Pradeep and his team for all the trips that I did. If it were not for the rural immersion trips that Mart was organizing on bespoke basis, these trips would never have happened. I also would like to highlight that the numerous occasions on which I met Pradeep and the several conversations we had on the Indian rural economy and state of affairs was responsible for piquing my interest in this subject as it sounded so fascinating and multi-layered that it was worth diving deeper into it.

I would also like to thank Alankrita Mahendra, my cousin sister who herself is a senior professional in the publishing world. Her constant guidance and encouragement to help me with the publishing process has been invaluable. Helping me reach out to publishers, guiding me on how to structure the initial parts before submitting to potential publishing houses was extremely useful. Alankrita has been always quick to respond to any query I had and even going out of the way to read the entire manuscript at short notice. The editorial inputs provided by her were all very meaningful.

And last but not the least, I would like to thank Vineet Nayar for having agreed to write the foreword to my book. I have known Vineet for a very long time but had not been in touch for many years. Hence it was nice to see that the old goodwill was still there and Vineet took out time to do this.

Dedication

Dedicated to the fond memory of my dear father – Dhanraj Pershad Sahgal, who passed away recently and was waiting anxiously for this book to see the light of day. He has always believed in living a full life and continuously striving for more and has had unending belief in his children which has given us so much self-confidence.

Dedicated to Veena, my wife and Saaz and Swar, my kids, who are the joy of my life and inspire and motivate me to keep moving up and achieving greater heights of fulfilment.

Disclaimer

This book contains sections and chapters which are full of comments and thoughts on Rural India. These were gathered as insights and observations from hundreds of interactions with people living in villages and working on the farms as well as various key opinion leaders. There are also statements made through the entire book which are based on what the author has read in general media on certain topics. Hence the author makes no claim to the factual accuracy of any of the data or information mentioned herein, although every effort has been made to check its validity. Much of the content is packaging of what I heard these people say. The reader should treat this as such — opinions, views, thoughts and perceptions rather than factual and accurate statements.

FOREWORD
By Vineet Nayar

Agriculture employs almost half of the country's population, but its contribution to GDP is merely 18%. No wonder then, farmers' suicides continued to hit the headlines even as India made rapid economic strides over the past two decades. The government's interventions such as increased support prices for various crops and farm loan waivers did provide short-term relief to farmers but have failed to tackle the root of the problem.

I gave up being the Vice Chairman and CEO of HCL Technologies in 2013 and started working full-time on innovative ideas to drive large-scale change in primary education, through Sampark Foundation. I travelled extensively through villages across Chhattisgarh, Jharkhand, Uttarakhand, Uttar Pradesh, Himachal and Haryana and it became clear that farmers were stuck in a primitive age. There is surprisingly low adoption of modern, innovative agricultural practices among farmers and poor awareness of schemes and resources available to help them; thus, the farmers' destinies remain tied to the vagaries of the weather.

The root of this problem is poor education—not so much the lack of educational infrastructure, but the quality of education.

An educated and informed farmer and his family can understand and manage the economics of agriculture better to improve farm output, profitability and his life. Our approach of using design thinking to bring to life frugal, innovative ideas across seventy-six thousand rural schools touching the lives of seven million children, has shown spectacular results in terms of increased learning outcomes and reduced dropout rates. Similar disruptive, inclusive and innovative ideas can also solve the unsolved problem in agriculture and kickstart our rural economy.

Sujit's book is a refreshing read and very timely because it gives an outsider's view that is not trapped by policy, history or theory. It is a traveller's perspective with deep insights on how to frame the problem to solve it. He has deftly combined a scholar's academic rigour, a banker's analytical skills and a journalist's reporting skills to provide a new, objective perspective on a wide range of issues facing farm economy in India. His insights into the various challenges and opportunities: roadblocks and the way-outs, will promote a better understanding among all stakeholders of what ails the farm sector and will help evolve ideas that could put agriculture back on a growth path. Sometimes an outsider's perspective is all we need to kickstart innovative ideas that drive change, and this is as good as it gets.

We need to understand that the country's economic growth will never be equitable unless the benefits reach rural India and we will never solve the rural problem, unless many others like Sujit decide to look at it closely and offer ideas and solutions as if it was 'their' problem.

Vineet Nayar
Founder Chairman
Sampark Foundation

INTRODUCTION

This book took its roots in late 2014 / early 2015 and I already titled it then without having written even a page. I spoke about it to all my friends and family and even my clients; as if speaking about it made me feel less guilty of procrastination. By late 2017 I had progressed... and now even had the cover artwork worked out... yes, still before having written a single word! So, the fact that you are reading this must mean I have since completed it and it truly has been a labour of love.

The genesis of my stories and experiences of rural India actually dates back to 2012. I used to be involved in equity investor conferences and at one of these conferences (February 2012) the rural theme was quite popular. Two speakers were invited to talk about rural India and the opportunity of how companies can and are, trying to target this large part of the economy. I heard both of them with lots of interest. Two of the most interesting insights I got from those talks was that there are multiple 'rural' Indias and one has to be clear about how you define it and secondly, that the lines between rural and urban are fast blurring with increasing consistency in between semi urban / semirural nomenclature. This piqued my interest and a month later when I was hosting a delegation of foreign investors, I suggested that we include a few hours of a "village visit" into the itinerary. It went very well, and I repeated it with a half day visit for another set of investors, this time in the peak of the Indian summer in late May.

There were several other such rural trips—only the trips got longer and more complex, covering more geographies, provinces, income levels and more slices of rural India. We kept peeling the onion to discover more interesting aspects and truths about rural life—many known already and some not so well known. Even the mix of participants got increasingly diverse. Men and women of all ages—twenties to their sixties—and from across the world: Americas, Europe and Asia have participated in these trips over the years. Soon a distinct pattern started to emerge, and a clear story was getting told. All I had to do was to connect the dots and put this into a flow of logical sequences. That's how the book was conceived.

So what follows is a smorgasbord of thoughts, observations and conclusions drawn from nearly a dozen rural trips conducted over the last seven years. It consists of maybe three hundred to four hundred interviews carried out with various participants of the rural economy. Starting from the simple, small farmer to his wife and children, all the way to the village chief as well as the local school principal and the friendly, local doctor as well as civil contractors and the not so friendly money lenders. It includes several visits to the local milk collection centres and dairies as well as *mandis* as well as the traditional and modern warehouses. Visits and interviews were also conducted with the entire retail economy at the feeder towns which included dealers of consumer durables and non-durables and give a picture of the consumption patterns of the farmer and his family. The footprint spread across Haryana, Uttar Pradesh, Uttarakhand, Rajasthan, Maharashtra, Madhya Pradesh and Tamil Nadu; a fair representation of the entire country for the most part. From these I have attempted to very broadly draw out realities of the rural economy of India, from the eyes of sophisticated foreign institutional investors, who have usually not known what to expect and have gone back with mixed conclusions of the near to medium term outlook; sometimes clearly a very positive one and sometimes not so positive, but always with this feeling as one of their most memorable experiences ever. Importantly as the host and the common denominator in all these trips, I was affected the most. Although being of Indian origin and having my fair share of growing up road trips and hence rural exposure, as well as watching the usual Bollywood fare which has centred around rural India so often, I still had so much to learn and be amazed with which I have tried to capture in this book.

It was like a new discovery for me although I was wearing a financial markets professional hat and the macroeconomic implications (rural incomes, wealth, demand) was centremost, the social aspects flared up quite often and even the philosophical aspects etched themselves in my memory.

I have contemplated hard how to present this book, or rather story, to make it readable and fun rather than yet another intense book on the financial markets or a boring book full of statistics and academic focus. I hope readers will like this *hybrid* style I have finally adopted, where I have blended the format between a diary-like narrative of a typical day on the road or a particularly touching interaction, with chapters dealing with topics that emerged from those interactions. This was also an idea I got from one of my friends while discussing the book.

The focus of these trips was clearly from a financial and macroeconomic perspective. Given the fact that the Indian rural economy employs two-thirds of the population and accounts for half of all consumption. This was an important piece of the puzzle for any long-term investor in India. The main areas of interest were: income and employment outlook for the farmer, what role loans are playing in his overall spending power and the spending preferences and patterns. This covered the entire scope of the interactions. It gave insights to the investors about what are the drivers of income (revenues and costs), how the financial sector is exposed to this segment (lending opportunity but also gauging asset quality) and finally where would they spend (education, autos, appliances, entertainment etc.) in times of scarcity or when things were better. This was from a near-term and a long-term perspective. To gauge the longer-term potential, areas like education and mechanisation as well as health and the generational shift were looked into. I had the opportunity to gauge the mood of rural populations towards the various changing government administrations whichever they were at the time. So, what actually started as a pure financial inquiry broadened to include important social aspects too and hence makes this a more interesting read for a far wider audience.

Pinch of Salt

Before we get into the details of understanding the farmer's world, a very important thing to be clear of is that there will be some responses from the villagers which are biased due to their own agenda. When an outsider visits a village and asks them about their income and their outlook, there will always be a high chance that many of the responses will be negative. A lot of negativity will be expressed in the hope that you would be the messenger or even the catalyst to change things for them. In perennial hope that even if some of us took the message back and happen to be in a position to influence change, they could get some of their needs met. After cross questioning a lot of the key opinion leaders in the village one is able to rip off the biases and get to the facts. On the flip side, sometimes there will be groups that will be overly positive about everything despite the facts pointing otherwise. This is part of any ground level interactions but they have their own value in terms of giving you an insight of what is motivating them and does not diminish the value of insights one gathers from such field trips.

I have divided this book into five main areas: earning and spending power (and I have spent considerable time on this.) The second part is about the bridge between the two, which is the borrowing and leverage. The third part is about the infrastructure which will enable higher earnings: the market structure & supply chain. The fourth part is more social; how attitudes towards education are changing and how women are coming out of the shadows and will drive much of the future and the last part is about the future of demographics; how urbanisation and access to information and opportunity can be a double-edged sword, without enabling reform for land aggregation or corporatisation of farming. Each chapter is preceded by a *trip diary* which narrates a highlight of the trip, which ties in with the topic of the following chapter. I have chosen five trips out of the nearly dozen I have done so far, based on something that stood out in each for me. Each area is further divided into smaller chapters to keep it punchy but at the same time provide adequate depth.

What makes this a differentiated and interesting read is that all these above topics were seen from the eyes of foreign institutional investors and is a culmination of not just my views and thoughts, but drawn from constant discussions with the hundreds of people from across the globe—from Japan to Australia to Canada to Korea—that were part of these trips. I hope you enjoy reading this book as much as I have enjoyed writing it, though I cannot promise you the same pleasure as I got while actually taking these trips! For that you have to join me next time…

Section One
Earning and Spending Power

The Very First Trip
Uttar Pradesh — Neemkheda village, Bulandshaher feeder town

We left the Imperial hotel, New Delhi around eleven in the morning in a bus full of people from all over the world. Last minute hiccups delayed us a little as I wanted to make sure the hotel had packed the right amount of lunch boxes so that we all had enough to eat on our way before we reached our stop. It was to be a two to three hour drive on our way to Agra where we were to stop at a village and spend approximately three hours in a "rural immersion" experience. This was my first trip of this kind, and I was a bit nervous because although I am of Indian origin, I had spent three quarters of my career outside India and had to remain sharp, so as not to give out some misinformation and sound very much the seasoned expert on not only India, but also rural India. We had taken the help of a rural marketing research consultancy as well as several friends and contacts in the two-wheeler tractor, agri-chemicals and banking industry, to help us set up an interesting bunch of meetings and interactions.

I still remember distinctly when the bus stopped at the edge of the highway just before a small lane that turned left, I could see the colourful, bright, fabric tent-like structure just by the side of the road, where some fifteen to twenty senior village folk: farmers and *sarpanch* (head of the local governing body, panchayat) were waiting for us patiently. (We were running around forty-five minutes late). The hosts had put up, as agreed, a line of tables and chairs (like a podium) where these "key opinion leaders" would sit and answer questions from the audience. (That was us.) The bus stopped and the fifteen to twenty of us walked out, clearly overwhelming the simple village folk as they had probably not seen so many foreign nationals coming to their village before; and that too, they were coming to actually speak and interact with many of them at close quarters. We spent an hour in that "tent" after which we proceeded for a "village walk". On the way one of the villagers showcased farms on both sides of the narrow road that we were walking on and showed us a pilot going on to demonstrate the efficacy of using various crop-protection inputs; and how it is not easy to convince farmers to spend the money unless they can really be convinced of the benefits, and the fact that "seeing is believing" for the farmers.

After a short walk through the village, we reached the village square "*choupal*". To our surprise, the village chief had arranged for *fresh milk* to be served in large stainless-steel cups as a sign of welcoming the guests and a mark of respect. Many of us were not expecting this (including me) and were not sure how to react. Our local friends told us to accept it and try the milk and that it would be okay, and that we would never have tasted such fresh, tasty, pure milk. Most of us did try it and actually loved it. It did taste nice and different from the UHT milk we have daily.

All this while we indulged in informal conversations with small groups of KOLs (key opinion leaders) who had stayed back with us to answer our questions. One of the lady guests with me got so affected by the positivity and spirit of these people, that she asked me how she could donate some money for the wellbeing of these villagers, and whether she could give them some money on the spot. I had to tell her that it is best to funnel it through a reputed NGO (non-governmental organisation) working in these areas or for certain causes and to not give them cash.

Trip Diary #1 — The Surprise Dance

We now were just wrapping up our discussions and started walking back towards our bus. We had to be conscious of time as the larger group had to reach Agra for a pre-fixed dinner by around seven, but before we could get onto to the bus we had a surprise waiting for us. A group of ten to fifteen women (young and old) had gathered to show us a local folk-dance performance, which is traditionally performed in their village on a festival which had just gone by. So to highlight that and welcome the guests they wanted to perform that again. It was absolutely unexpected and unknown to me and I was not sure how to react. We watched with great awe; how the women danced and how many of my guests joined in the dancing and loved it. I remember distinctly one of the conversations about inter-village marriages and how they were very rare and actually explicitly discouraged. The day had been fruitful with some very interesting discussions on the basics. The farmers' income and spending patterns in the recent past and their expectations of the near future…

CHAPTER 1
Understanding the Farmer's Income

Historical Context

Currently the Indian per capita rural income is around Rs6500 per month. In the 2017 financial year budget the government pledged to double this by March 2022. A few years ago, farmers' incomes had gone up quite a bit due to a few short-term reasons. 1) The government had hiked the minimum support prices (MSP) by a hefty 30 to 40% per year. The MSP is the floor price fixed by the government at which it will procure certain grains, cereals, pulses etc. on a yearly basis. A roaring bull market in global soft commodities as well as a generally weakening rupee also helped keep the MSPs high, to the extent they were linked to landed prices. 2) Over and above this, the government had announced a massive income guarantee programme which guaranteed an income of Rs100 per day for one hundred days, to every rural household. A policy to boost demand. The government launched projects (roads, local infrastructure, buildings etc.) for which they enrolled workers who showed up to work with a "logbook", where they recorded how many days of work they had done. Periodically this logbook would be added up and the local administrator would pay them their dues through a direct benefit transfer (DBT) into their bank account. (Yes, the government had a big financial inclusion drive going on as well.) At the peak of the NREGA (National Rural Employment Guarantee Act) project flow, earnings from this programme alone were approximately 30% of monthly household income. 3) At the same time, from 2009 to 2013 post the financial crisis, asset price inflation was rampant with land prices and gold prices booming. Many industrial groups were setting up projects and acquiring land from farmers at hefty prices. Many farmers sold land to boost short term "wealth" only to squander it away in consumption and realised soon that they were rendered landless, without any sustainable source of income

Gold prices were also going up or at least were firm at high levels and added to the wealth effect. This was a heady cocktail for anyone to resist. So, it was a significant boost to income and spending power. As will be explained later, all the four situations have in the last four to five years moved in the opposite direction and reversed this feeling of rural prosperity.

So far, the government seems to have focused on short term solutions to boost the farmers' income (NREGA and high MSP hikes) which actually either hiked farm labour costs, skewed crop selection or caused inflation. More structural and longer-term solutions are required to inherently improve the underlying earning power of the farmers. Some of the recent initiatives and announcements (crop and health protection) protect income and savings and improve the economic structure of the farmer. Spreading the MSP applicability to more / all crops and allowing world class processes to be used in cultivation (size, inputs, mechanisation and irrigation) will go a long way.

Understanding the Farmer's Income and Its Sources

The government of India wants to double farmer incomes by 2022. The key areas to focus on, at the cost of sounding too simplistic, would be volume of products and their prices. Volumes are driven by the acreage (farm size), the kind of and number of crops grown and the yield the farmer gets. Pricing in India works through two mechanisms. The market determined price the farmer gets at the *Mandi* and the minimum support price that the government is willing to pay to procure for the public distribution system (ration shops) or to protect the farmer from low prices. On the one hand market prices often fall below the MSP and due to lack of storage infrastructure the farmer is forced to sell at the clearing price of the day, as he also does not have the pricing information of other *mandis* nearby. On the other hand, the government through FCI (Food Corporation of India) is not really able to procure all the quantity offered at the promised MSP for lack of infrastructure.

A farmer's primary farm income depends on a few key things, and it is worth exploring each of the topics.

Size of Farm Holdings and How They Are Shrinking

The starting point of what a farmer earns is clearly based on how much cultivable land he owns. The farmers in India start off with a disadvantage on this front due to very small average land holdings of just under three acres. By global standards this is very low as the average in other countries is closer to one hundred acres, if not more. The entire European Union has an average of around forty acres with most larger countries being above one hundred. In the US it is a whopping four hundred and forty acres. China is actually an exception with half the size of Indian holdings but 30 to 40% higher production. This does not stop here as this trend of dwindling holdings is continuing as the land passes from the head of the family to his children. A farmer owning ten acres passes it to his two sons (five acres each) who then pass it to their next generation of two or three children and they are left with just one and a half acres each; below the current national average thus pulling it down further, and so on and so forth. This is and will remain the most important point to understand as everything else is hostage to the farm holding size. This trend of dropping farm holdings has been observed in other parts of the world too, so though not a unique phenomenon it is nevertheless important to tackle. Low farm holdings lead to much lower yields as investments in irrigations, seeds, storage and mechanisation are not viable.

The easiest thing would be to allow a corporate to lease land and do contract farming with all the benefits of modern technology. Corporate farming was tried in India but was not seen to be politically palatable and was disallowed. Land aggregation under contract farming by farmers is allowed. Laws on these are not still very clear but even where they are, there are two bottlenecks.

1) The entrepreneurial farmers who will come forward to aggregate the land by leasing in the farms of his fellow farmers are few and far between. (About 10% of farmers only.) This is because farming in India is seen as a subsistence living with many moving parts and is not seen as a risk worth taking with so many variables and no safety nets (weather, prices, storage, insurance etc.). The farmer is not clear whether in the next few crop seasons he will be able to make enough money after paying the fixed price per acre to the landowner.

2) The landowner himself is not usually comfortable or willing to lease out his land due to a severe lack of trust between fellow farmers as well as not wanting to see someone become big and successful. (Only 5% of Farmers do it!) Once some of these issues are fixed or addressed, India can see its average farm holding go up, leading to much higher yields.

Choice of Crops and Single Versus Dual Cropping

The second most important part that determines a farmer's income is what crop he is growing and whether he is growing one or two crops in a year. Not all farmers in a particular area need to grow the same crops (weather, soil etc.), but they tend to do that. Most farmers also grow only one crop a year but are beginning to adopt dual crop farming. Actually, certain crops do not allow for dual cropping (i.e. the cropping cycle is so long that it does not leave time for a second crop). So, in a way the choice, or lack of it, of which crop a farmer grows determines whether he grows one or two cycles. The crop decision should logically and ideally be driven by (apart from weather and soil) its profitability too, which would be determined by its yields and pricing, just in the same way as a businessman would make his capital allocation. But the farmer is very risk averse and prefers to go with a choice which is least risky. He ends up choosing the crop which is backed by the government procurement programme — the MSP. This pricing mechanism has led to farmers all drifting towards those crops that have an MSP and avoiding higher yielding, higher profitability crops as they come with no guaranteed prices. The few farmers (you meet one or two in every village) who took the initiative have had a much better economic outcome than the others. Risk and reward go hand in hand. But the skew that the MSP policy causes in crop choice is quite apparent.

The government actually intended to have a minimum support price for a large list of crops, but it really became an effective policy for only two main crops — paddy and wheat. This led most farmers to disproportionately cultivate these two crops. The area under cultivation for these kept growing, which actually backfired in the sense that it created oversupply and lower prices. Several discussions with farmer groups brings this out very clearly. This is most apparent in the choice between growing much more profitable fruits and vegetables versus food grains or pulses. The former are more perishable and come with no support or guarantee of purchase by the government. The lack of a cold chain renders horticulture even less attractive. To reduce this skew, the government over the years have increased the number of crops included in the MSP program, but it still effectively only covers a limited number of crops.

Multi-cropping needs a lot of focus and resources. The farmer has to choose the crop with the faster growing time and also a mix of crops which need more water and less water, i.e. complimentary crops. Sometimes to manage closely scheduled harvesting and sowing periods, higher investments in technology (drying moist harvest, faster preparation of the soil etc.) or storage is required. None of this is common given the small and marginal nature of farming in the country, making it a vicious cycle. The second aspect is that usually grains like paddy take the longest time to grow (one hundred and ten days), vegetables take a bit less (ninety days) while fruits take the least (forty-five days). So, in reality, dual cropping to a large extent presupposes horticultural exposure, so the farmer has to be willing to grow horticultural crops and take the risk (no MSP or government procurement). Most will stick to paddy and wheat cycles as both fall under the MSP program. It also needs a strong irrigation system / water availability and hence by definition, only certain parts of the country have farmers practicing this.

This habit or herd mentality sometimes is so entrenched that I have visited several villages in Western Uttar Pradesh where the main crop grown was sugarcane and the mill in their catchment area, to which they had to sell was making losses and was not paying them for a few years. Yet they still were not willing to try out a different crop, hoping that soon the mills would make their full payments. This is a common problem in the sugarcane belt when there is a bumper crop and sugar prices fall. The mills start losing money and hence delay payments to farmers. Recently the UP-cane farmers were only paid 60% of their dues while the rest were held back.

Monsoon Affects Production Volumes

Monsoons are synonymous with the rural economy and prosperity, especially in India. It is taken as a given that a bad monsoon means a bad crop for the farmers. This inherently makes farming an extremely unpredictable commercial activity and hence needs very complex solutions to protect farm incomes.

Monsoons have been tricky in India for the last several years. Droughts get reported and talked about when the quantity of rainfall is way below the long-term average but that is not the only thing that matters. The spatial distribution and timing of rainfall is equally important. So, while the whole country may get a normal monsoon (+/- 5% of average), several agricultural states may receive much lower. Secondly, if the monsoon timing is erratic — starting earlier or ending late — it also affects the crops. This indeed has been the case for last several years, with one of the three conditions not being aligned: quantity, timing or spatial distribution. Hence rendering farmers in a tough spot. The volatility of rural incomes and its linkage to rains can be seen from the fact that just a bout of unseasonal rains was responsible for almost a 40% drop in sales of utility vehicles in parts of rural Maharashtra in 2015. This linkage is due to the damage unseasonal rain does to standing crops.

Global changes in temperature are clearly affecting farmers in India too. The rains getting more erratic, delayed, or unseasonal have rendered the farmers increasingly at the mercy of policy makers for a more sustainable and reliable economics. No wonder also that there is low interest in younger generations to stick to this activity. That brings me to the next part of the monsoon discussion as well as to some analysis on how dependent food grain production is on rains.

Many of the government schemes providing support to drought-ridden farmers are very rule-oriented and get into technicalities, thus preventing many from getting the support they actually deserve. Regions where the monsoon has been normal or even good may still suffer from bad growing conditions because the connectivity of the river water to the farm may not be adequate. Canals are required to be built from the river to the farms and if these are not built then despite a good rainfall, famers may suffer. Secondly sometimes the farms are located at long distances from the rivers and the canal infrastructure may not reach all key farming areas.

Irrigation Levels Are Rising but Not Enough to Break the Link Yet

The second most important phenomenon is the low levels of irrigation in India which keeps the farmers' dependence on the rain gods uncomfortably high. Although irrigation penetration has been increasing over the years and is close to 36% still a majority of the farms depend on the rain gods. Hence, a farmer's income remains very volatile and fragile. Just because it is nearly twice the global average (21% global, 40% in Asia) does not mean this is not a problem for India as globally the need for irrigation is low due to natural weather conditions and precipitation levels.

On the other hand, the very connection between monsoons and rural prosperity is often questioned because correlation between rainfall normalcy and food grain production growth appears low at times or completely absent. The belief that with low irrigation penetration, crop output and the farmer are hostage to the monsoon, gets diluted considering that actually India has witnessed a continuous rise in grain production through good and bad monsoons over the last several years

There maybe two reasons for this low correlation between the two. One is that the definition of food grains mainly includes wheat and rice which make up 70 to 80% of the food grains (approximately 200mt of 260mt), and it does not include other agricultural produce like fruits, vegetables and most cash crops. Secondly the pan-India rainfall does not tell the whole story as mentioned above and a 106% monsoon may be worse than a 95% one and vice versa as visible below. So, although there is progress going on in irrigation, higher yielding seeds, farm mechanisation etc. it may be premature to say that the link to monsoons is coming down.

Year	Output mt	Rain	Production growth
FY11	244.49	102%%	+12%
FY12	259.29	93%	+6%
FY13	257.13	106%%	+0%
FY14	265.04	88%	+3%
FY15	252.02	86%	-4.9%
FY16	251.57	97%	+0%
FY17	275.68	95%	+9.6%

Source: Agricultural Statistics Division, Directorate of Economics & Statistics as on 16.08.2017, Department of Agriculture, Cooperation and Farmers welfare Fourth Advance Estimates of Production of Foodgrains for 2016-17, IMD annual monsoon reports

Crop Insurance Can Help to Protect Income

In a country with small land holdings, erratic monsoon and still low irrigation levels, a very powerful and necessary solution is crop insurance. In such a cover, the farmer gets paid if he loses the farm output due to bad weather or infection (pest attack). The protection can be based on either the evidence of the occurrence of one of these events (low rains or a pest attack) or based on just the loss of production yields. Historically India has had crop protection schemes which were focused on evidence of the reason. This was found to be less effective in honouring the farmers' claims when they needed it most. So recently (2014) the government announced a change in the scheme dynamics and linked the protection to crop output drop. The scheme has been widely advertised and the government has a lofty target of getting 50% of all farmers under this scheme by 2020. Currently around a third of the farmers are supposed to be already part of this scheme. However, over several farm visits and discussions it appears that all is not well.

A well-intentioned scheme has had hiccups in implementation. The local panchayat chief has to, along with the *patidar*, assess the damage and file the case. As insurance has now moved from weather-based (quantity of rainfall) to yield-based (loss of quantity of production), claims are not passed unless all contiguous areas have the same problem. Often, local farmers are not aware of scheme deadlines to register themselves — an example of information scarcity.

Pricing and Market Access

Once the farmer has the land, the right crop mix and has been gifted with some decent rains or access to irrigation, the next important step is to get this produce to the market and get the right price for it. The government has a set-up of the Agricultural Produce Market Committee (APMC) which are basically *mandis* where the farmer can go and sell his produce on a daily basis. The APMC has registered broker agents who buy on behalf of their customers, who could be consumer companies, processors or exporters. The system of buying is on an open auction basis and the farmer has to agree to sell at the highest bid at the auction.

The other mechanism that the government runs is that of

the MSP – which we have spoken about above. The government procures food grains for the public distribution system as well as for strategic reserves and stores it in its warehouses owned by the Food Corporation of India (FCI). In theory roughly twenty-three crops are covered under this MSP mechanism: seven cereals, five pulses, eight oilseeds and a few other crops like coconut, cotton and jute. In reality though the government has been effectively applying it to only a few kharif and rabi crops but has been increasing its scope lately. Sadly, the infrastructure to procure even those limited crops does not exist. It is also going a step further to see if it can supplement the existing APMC infra (bringing twenty-two thousand village *haats* under the APMC umbrella) and pay the farmer just the difference if the mandi prices are lower than the MSPs. This is called the *Bhavantar Yojana* in some states as it promises to pay the difference.

So, all along the MSP has been the main mechanism of solving the farmers' income problem. Though fixed based on cost assessment by the Committee on Agricultural Costs & Prices (CACP), the government had flexibility and it could adjust and fine tune the price levels based on the state of the rural economy. This approach to solve rural income problems is not sustainable and could change with changes in the government and their philosophies. The UPA administration supported by high-global, soft commodity prices had hiked the MSPs by 30-40% in some cases for several years. It was these high and repeated hikes for several years that created an artificial sense of rural income buoyancy and also got farmers hooked onto an elevated level of consumption; a habit with long term repercussions as discussed in the section on rising rural leverage. High MSPs also led to a rise in food inflation.

The government resolve to curb inflation was helped by the timely softening of global soft commodity prices. Hence MSP hikes became very small or negligible in the last few years.

While the pricing part has been kept benign for the last many years, the access part has been a trouble spot. The problem lies in the basic concept that the farmer gets a fraction of what you and I pay for his produce and that one way of improving his income, all else being equal, is to just reduce or remove the fat margin that the middlemen take away. One of the reasons why a farmer realises less than fair price for his produce is the lack of transparent grading at the *Mandi*. Which means either receiving a low price for a standard quality product or getting the standard price for a premium quality product. Payment cycles of how soon the farmer would get paid for the produce, was also at the mercy of the agents. So, getting the right price and getting paid early have been two problems facing the farmers. The other issue has been distance of these mandis from the village. If they are too far and the farmer is marginal — with a small quantity to sell, it is seldom viable for him to hire transportation to go all the way to sell it. He would end up selling it to local aggregators who would buy produce from several farmers (could be the representative of the *adatiya* as well) and take it to the *mandi* instead. The price difference the farmer would get would usually be perceived to offset the extra cost of transportation and value of time spent on the travel. As the produce is perishable or requires large storage areas, the farmer does not have any bargaining power and usually lets his wares sell at the price the agents are quoting at the farm gate, whether it is fair or not.

Information dissemination of prices per grade across nearby *mandis* is crucial so the farmer can be aware and choose to take his produce to another *mandi* if he sees a better price. Efforts have been made to make available real time prices for key crops to the farmers through electronic terminals (ITC — eChoupal) some years ago and more broadly via smartphones now.

Storage and Efficient Working Capital Financing

This is where the importance of proper storage facilities comes through and we will discuss this at length in a separate section. In the past the only storage facilities were the FCI godowns owned by the government. These were not really available to the farmer and were used by the government for its strategic storage. So, the farmer had to rely on small unorganised players if there were any. Lately a few private players have entered the warehousing space and while they mainly store for the buyer, they can also store for the seller. More than just storing in a safe place (India loses a third of its agricultural produce to theft, rodents and weather), they would also grade it in a lab and based on a warehouse receipt, the farmer could actually borrow against such stock, hence not needing to sell if market prices were abnormally low. This again could boost the income of the farmer without the government using tactical MSP, which is more expensive for the government. We visited several of these modern warehouses as well as the FCI godowns. The contrast is stark. The new infrastructure is very impressive in terms of quality of construction, well-lit clean spaces, with security and pest control to prevent rodents from coming in. The only problem is that most of them cater to the buyers and not the sellers. Even when a warehouse owner is willing to offer his service to a farmer, the farmers are not fully aware of what is on offer. In one instance I was told that a few years ago only 5% of their customers were sellers but currently nearly one in five are the selling farmers, as awareness improves. This reinforces one of my strongest observations, which is information scarcity. Not many farmers know that they can store their produce at a reasonable cost and even get financing against it.

Awareness — The Under Appreciated Solution

One of the most important realisations of these visits and discussions is that of information scarcity in the villages. More than giving doles or short-term fixes to farmers, a much higher return on effort could be by disseminating timely information with the right amount of details to the right people. This would make them aware of the various schemes available to them and how they can benefit from them. Rather than keeping on launching new schemes every few years it would be better to educate the farmer on the existing ones and increase their utilisation. Never have I met a group of farmers or villagers that were clear or in sync about a particular scheme. In the same room, we got different answers about factual things we were asking about, whether it was crop insurance, DBT, NREGA, *Jandhan* accounts or newer schemes about MSP pricing, Health insurance and subsidies for solar powered irrigation pumps or access to storage facilities. There are so many layers of scheme administration that the message gets lost in transit at its best and is intentionally kept blurred at its worst. A private market research firm with its field staff can make a big difference by spreading the right information about the key government policies and schemes, I often feel. The frustration and anger it causes among farmers is tangible and completely unnecessary. I have often heard stories of farmers believing they are eligible for some benefits (crop insurance or farm loan waiver for example) and going to the people in charge for their claims during time of need, only to be told that the scheme is not applicable to him for various reasons (either he does not fall in the definition of the farm loan waiver or he forgot to register his land so cannot claim crop insurance etc.) This is getting too frequent. Hence it is no surprise that on the one hand the farmer feels neglected while on the other hand, the government thinks it is doing so much.

Cost Economics at The Farm

Income growth of the farmer is a combination of what he makes by selling his produce and what it costs him to produce that. Though it may sound like economics 101, it's often forgotten by people who are supposed to follow the farm economy closely and even by experts. Higher output or higher prices are seen as enough to ensure increased profitability and income. Market economists also feel this will mean more spending power, without giving due recognition to the other important element which is the costs involved. Hence, I have devoted a small sub-chapter to this topic.

Input Costs

Theoretically as explained above, the MSP is fixed based on costs, so one can argue that it is in the most part self-correcting. But the reality is that not much margin is priced into these calculations, the market prices are usually below the MSP and hence it is really only 'on paper'. Again, only a fraction of crops grown by farmers are under the MSP ambit. In many years even when the MSPs have risen a fair bit, costs of production have been rising faster for the farmers on several counts and this got pronounced in years with small or no price hikes. The key component of the costs can be divided into three categories. The actual or direct out of pocket cost a farmer bears, for the seeds, fertilisers and pesticides, farm labour as well as power cost to run the pumps for pulling out the water from below the surface. The second part of the cost is the imputed cost of family labour that is involved in farming. The last part of the cost includes imputed cost of capital and land that the farmer owns / deploys. Our discussion below will focus on the direct costs.

Labour

One of the key costs out of these, is the wages paid to the farm labour. 1) Due to the progressive urbanisation, farm labour is slowly migrating to the cities and nearby towns and causing a shortage. This has led to their charges going up. 2) The NREGA scheme where the government was guaranteeing nearly Rs100 per day for fairly passive work, pushed up the prices for farm labour too and a large chunk of labourers preferred just surviving on the minimum guarantee work which reduced their supply even more. Over the years the NREGA wages have gone up to Rs160 a day and this has pushed up the farm wages to nearly Rs300 to 350 a day. This is expensive for a farmer. In fact, there is an interesting link between labour costs and use of herbicides. High farm labour costs are actually encouraging use of herbicides as the cost of manually removing the herbs is far more than spraying the new age herbicides.

Power

Most farms in India get their water supply through tube wells or bore wells. These are below ground wells sourcing water from the aquifer which has to be brought up by a pump. Furthermore, energy is required if you are deploying sprinklers as a form of irrigation. Currently in most parts of India the farmer does not have a meter at his receiving point, and hence the power supplier cannot calculate the quantity of power he has used. They pay a lumpsum based on the capacity of the pump (Rs500 per month per 10 kWh motor). Farmers agree they have it lucky on this front but also highlight the fact that they barely get five to six hours of power a day in most provinces (states) and many times a good part of this availability is during the night! They are happy to pay based on consumption if they get uninterrupted power when they want it. Central and state governments have made efforts to upgrade the distribution infrastructure and install meters which will help identify farm level consumption. It remains to be seen how soon this happens and how it impacts farmer costs further.

Seeds and Chemicals

The farmer uses seeds as a key input and chemicals like fertilisers to provide good nutrients to the soil for better crop growth. He also has to add crop protection chemicals against pests, fungus and parasitical herbs that grow around the crop and suck out the nutrients. Farmers have regularly highlighted the general rise in costs of seeds as they increasingly use more advanced hybrid seeds for better yields. This entire complex of chemical is another important part of his costs. Over the years, better education by the government and company sales forces has led to higher adoption and use of these chemicals. In addition to higher usage, their prices have also been going up. Another interesting observation here is that with increased marketing and branding as well as larger field sales forces, the branded companies have been pushing the benefit of using protection as well as their brand benefits. This has led to a significant increase in the consumption of branded chemicals. Five years ago 20% of farmers would ask for a pesticide by brand but today around 50% do so. Nearly half of them are willing to wait a while if their choice is not available. This has added to their costs as they are buying more and more expensive chemicals. This is also driven by the change in the behaviour of the farmer where he wants to adopt best practices and sometimes spends money, even if his crops do not have infection, just because his neighbour is doing so. This is all also adding to the cost. Here the soil card concept of the government is a good one, where the government conducts a soil test at each farm and based on the soil structure recommends a mix of fertiliser use. This will prevent farmers from using the cheapest fertiliser or over-using it just to emulate someone. Again, most farmers we spoke to were not very clear of this card and when they would get it.

Tractors

As most farmers in India are small and marginal (approximately 80%) and have just one to two acres of land, they cannot afford to own a tractor for themselves. Some studies have shown that only 25% of farmers own a tractor of their own. The rest hire a tractor as and when they need it and pay up to Rs600 per hour for tilling the land before sowing the seeds. This cost has been moving up and they do not have much bargaining power as well.

Grazing Land

Many farmers still use bullocks to till the land. Breeding cattle has also been a side activity for farmers to add to their income. In the past, grazing lands were freely available to farmers to feed their cattle (it was considered common, panchayat land). In recent years, the government has disallowed this in some states and the farmer has to pay for the cattle fodder plus, as stray cattle can't access the pastures they try to feed on the standing crops as well. This has added to his costs and hassle for the farmer.

In Conclusion

So overall while the major focus is on the revenues of the farmer, and rightfully so, a fair amount of importance has to be given to the costs as well. Adequate understanding and planning are required to make sure costs do not rise in line with price improvement, to offset any benefits that can be derived from there. This is actually a problem which is rarely discussed. That if the two are not solved in tandem, all the great work on the pricing and realisations for farmers can be undone if costs are not controlled, and the first step for that is to monitor them.

One of the big issues over the years has been that while

the media reported the hikes in MSPs or good monsoons leading to higher output (and hence implying rural prosperity), what was actually missed was that costs had been rising for farmers at various levels and this offset the positives to a meaningful extent. This is why input inflation hurts the farmer but usually goes unnoticed. We heard this complaint from the farmers on almost every village visit. But many an election has seen swings in fortunes due to the *mehangai* (inflation) and it is no surprise why. This is also the reason for the government's recent focus on fixing the MSP with a margin-based approach (50% above costs).

Direct Income Support — The Final Frontier?

Even while we were touring the villages and talk of higher MSP was going on, as well as that of the farm loan waiver, a new theme had taken control of the narrative due to logistical challenges of various schemes. That of direct income support as a third layer of support for the farmer (subsidies, support prices and now income support). The idea was to pay cash to farmers directly based on the cost of certain input items on a per acre basis (to buy seeds, pesticides etc.). This is not something new but was started successfully by one of the southern states — Telangana, called the *Rythu Bandhu*, which means "for my farmer friend". Telangana has six million farmers and around fourteen million acres of farmland. Each farmer (without any conditions) will get Rs4000 per season (Rs8000 per year) per acre via a cheque. This amount has been estimated based on the cost of cultivation i.e. spends on out of pocket expenses like seeds, pesticides and other incidentals. This is going to cost the state government Rs120bn per year.

This scheme had its short comings as it did not cover anyone who did not own land and would benefit the larger farmers more. Orissa then announced another scheme called the *Kalia* scheme, under which it gives Rs10000 per year to all farmers regardless of whether they own any land, and it is not linked to the quantity of land owned. It is a flat sum. They have budgeted Rs35bn per year to cover a million farmers and cultivators. On top of this the central government has announced its own PM-Kisan scheme which gives Rs6000 per year flat to any farmer who owns less than five acres of land; targeting one hundred and twenty million, of the one hundred and fifty million farmers in India. This is going to cost the centre Rs750bn. Last but not the least, the leading opposition party had announced its own election promise; Minimum Income Guarantee to the landless and small and marginal farmers but it had not etched out the details. So, to borrow a phrase from my colleague, it is clear that this train has definitively left the station and there is no turning back. It can only grow larger. The biggest problem with such targeted schemes is that proper land ownership records are a must to enrol the eligible people. The end use of this money will also not be tracked but economists prefer this method of support versus subsidies, which create distortions in pricing and resource allocation as well as demand. So, while it may be a better way to give support among all the other options, making farming inherently more profitable is the nirvana that will take some time. In the meantime, such handouts should not breed complacency among the farmers to do less rather than more.

Trip Diary #2 — NREGA Worker

It was a very hot summer afternoon and we were a small group of five. We had just finished the main open house session in the village school compound. In another room next door a few men were waiting for us, clutching small passbook-style books in their hands. It was nearly lunch time and we were in a rush, but this group was special. It was the first time we were going to actually physically meet some NREGA workers and hear from them what it has meant to them. So, I pulled my guests into the room promising them a fruitful and eye-opening discussion; and indeed, it was. The men were very thin, almost looking sick and could barely stand and speak to us. They were very shy too. One of them — Bajja Bhai was probably the most outspoken and took the initiative in speaking to us. He told us that in the last few years he was regularly working the designated one hundred days every year. I asked him what sort of work he was doing, and it was mainly digging pits outside the village for drainage or building some walls around farms and of course helping with road building. I asked him to show me his "logbook". I struggled to find any entry in it for the few hundred days he had supposedly worked. I finally counted some thirty to forty entries across years. He said that his old logbook has more data in it. I then asked him how he got paid for it. He said once the supervisor signed off on the attendance on a monthly basis, they get paid for the days worked. But there are lot of delays in getting the payment. I asked him if he is currently working on any projects and Bajja said he had not worked for a few months and has not heard of any projects on the anvil either, but that last few years this source of income had been very helpful.

CHAPTER 2
NREGA and Other Sources of Rural Employment

Overall it would be fair to say that the employment situation in rural India is pretty weak. Although there are several means of employment other than farming itself, some of the observations indicate that while there are patches of positivity, there is still a lot of potential to employ the rural youth.

Spotting Underemployment

On almost every visit to a village just before we alight at the village square for our first meeting, one gets a flavour of the life of the youth in the village. You will see dozens of young men between eighteen and twenty-five years of age hanging around and doing nothing. Someone once asked me if they were just gathering around due to curiosity about our visit. I have given them two responses: "What did you think people mean by disguised underemployment?", which drew a lot of laughs, and the other that its part curiosity and part slack period during a normal day in a farmer's life, but the truth really lies somewhere in the middle and makes the topic of rural unemployment very important to understand. Many youths are qualified but do not get government or private sector jobs. A recent trip brought out this aspect of the current government's failure to generate jobs. They do not want to work on their farms either because small holdings do not warrant much labour or because they do not belong to land-owning families. This hidden unemployment can be addressed by vocational training centres like the ones ITI (Industrial Training Institute) run, or even private sector-run English-speaking coaching classes. Success rates of such programs is not clear and needs to be assessed so that it does not become a scam. Attracting private sector into vocational training is also important, but having said this there are several sources of income for a villager other than being a land-owning farmer.

Sleepy Afternoons

Another way in which this hidden unemployment manifests itself is the very strange observation that in almost every village we visit, most of the small retail shops are shut for a very large part of the day. We have driven and walked through these at all times of the day -from eleven a.m. to five p.m., and we have noticed this almost every time. One of the reasons of course, is maybe the very narrow band of time during which the villagers come out to shop but it also points to the overall lack of demand and hence lack of need to be open for long.

Countless Vocational Centres

The other giveaway or red flag is something you spot way before even entering the village. Three to five kilometres before you reach the village, signs and hoardings on both sides of the road welcome you. These are for innumerable coaching centres for spoken English, interviewing and presentation skills and other vocational courses. They seem to be thriving — another sign of the challenged, rural employment opportunities. But this also has a positive angle to it. That younger villagers are keenly pursuing such skills to improve their lives.

NREGA Projects

Back in 2005 the incumbent government announced a national rural employment guarantee scheme (MNREGS). This was with the backdrop of a few drought years and suffering farmers, as well as a political move to appease the rural vote bank. The scheme was the mother of all Keynesian implementations where the government promised one hundred days of work to every poor household, paying them wages of Rs100 per day. The scheme was implemented in phases until 2008. This included women workers and also allowed more than one person from a household, if it were a husband and wife combination. Most logbooks I inspected across villages and time periods rarely showed the run rate of one hundred days per year, but on average workers were getting around forty to sixty days of work. Initially the payment for this would be in cash and released by the local administrator once every few months. There were cases of lots of delays in payments and some stories of the workers signing off on moneys never paid. On the other hand, there has been speculation that many labourers got paid without ever even showing up at the work site. It was allegedly a win-win situation where the administrator showed the full one hundred days of work done and pays the villager for fifty days (sometimes for no work done) and pockets the rest. All this of course, came to an end when the Congress government initiated Direct Benefit Transfer (DBT) schemes, which the current government took to the next level by opening hundreds of millions of accounts in a period of six to twelve months. Since then all payments are made within two weeks and are made directly into the bank account of the worker.

These NREGA projects started slowing down in mid to late 2014 just after the new BJP (Bharatiya Janata Party) / NDA (National Democratic Alliance) government came into power; or at least that's the perception of the farmers since they did not see a strong pipeline of projects. One of the reasons may have been a bit of a rethink on the kind of work being undertaken in this scheme. There was a need to make sure this was not wasted labour, literally digging and filing up pits, but being used for building much needed rural infrastructure like roads, bridges, toilets and *pucca* houses etc.

At the peak (2012-2014) this became a very material part of the monthly household income. By one estimate it was around 30% of the farmer's income; hence it was a critical boost. This was helpful when the few bad monsoons or lower MSP hikes occurred. However, this outside support could not last too long. The overall budget allocation by the central government for NREGA projects which started at around Rs400-500bn, dropped to Rs350bn and has now stabilised at around Rs580-600bn. This is because of government fiscal constraints. Moreover, the farm work daily wages are almost double what NREGA projects pay and hence demand for this is also going down (Rs300 a day versus Rs160). That is not a bad thing in itself but until all the workers find work on the farms, their income is surely dented.

Landless Labour

Not all the villagers or people employed in the farm sector are landowners. In fact, as per the statistics there are around one hundred to one hundred and twenty million farmers in India but there are nearly six hundred million people working in the agricultural sector. This clearly means that a very large number of people in the rural economy are landless, farm labourers. Often our discussions and analysis of the rural economy focuses mostly on the farmer as a landlord while actually most of the rural economy is driven by the landless labourers.

Construction Work

As mentioned later in this book, one of the key areas of spending for the villager is on home improvement. The local panchayat — the local governing body also keeps applying for projects to the local administration and gets a fair number of projects approved to build roads, build canals, drainage systems, hospitals and schools etc. Lastly, the central government has taken the initiative of adding rural roads, toilets and converting *kuccha* houses to *pucca* ones. All this throws up a lot of civil construction work which is taken up by small, local contractors. They are looking for slightly skilled labourers and are able to pay somewhat more than the farm labour rates and much more than the NREGA projects. In many villages I went to, the contractors were finding it difficult to get good quality labour but in the same village we also met dozens of labourers complaining about the lack of NREGA work, but not enrolling themselves with the contractor where they could earn two times the wage. This is another very important realisation that actually if village leaders are progressive and enthusiastic, even within the problematic weak economics of farming life, there is plenty of opportunity to get gainful employment and improve their livelihood. There is an interesting pattern visible — where certain villages in certain states are clearly more progressive and optimistic and some (in similar states) are not. Good local leadership can make a big difference.

Lack of Government Jobs

It was on one of my most recent trips that this point got reinforced. Usually villagers will always have some criticism of the government but this point that they brought up reminded me of a trip I had made three years ago, where a very similar issue had been raised. Over the years apparently government jobs have been an important supplement to the rural employment story. Every year a few dozen jobs would come up and absorb several young people from each village. Since the new government (BJP / NDA) came to power, they have focused on reducing red tape, bureaucracy and driving more governance with less government. This has led to much fewer jobs than in the past. In some cases, villages had almost no government jobs for the last year or two. This was not something I had heard often and hence made it a more credible complaint.

The Job Opportunity Cliff and The Steep Prosperity Curve

Having visited villages of all income groups and prosperity one of the interesting observations has been around the steepness of the prosperity curve. Villages which are within a 50 to 100 kilometre radius of a big city enjoy a very different level of income and prosperity due to the proximity of schools and job opportunities in the city. The moment one travels 150 to 200 kilometres from a city, the fall in the level of prosperity is very sharp, extremely evident and tangible. One would expect a more gradual fall as you go into the interiors, but the fall is stark and it again shows that most of the prosperity you experience may be less due to the farming buoyancy and more coming just from the village's proximity to a big city. Sad but quite true.

Land Acquisition and Its Pitfalls

During the boom years of the mid to late 2000s, lots of industrial activity was going on and businesses were trying to expand and put up capacity. Power projects, expressways, townships, free trade zones and industrial estates were all being planned at a frenetic pace. The farmers' land was bid up and many of them, given the vulnerability of their livelihoods, agreed to sell it off to the government or private industrialists. On the one hand the proceeds made them feel richer and boost their feel-good factor and hence their propensity to spend, but on the other hand it renders them landless and without a long-term source of employment. Many such farmers were promised jobs for their children when the new industrial estates came up. Many of these estates have been delayed significantly and those that have come through haven't lived up to their promises.

Farmer Mobility

It is also quite common that a farmer would sell his land at a good price and in exchange buy land a few hours away from his home. He would then manage the farming operations by travelling to this new location a few times a week and also employing lots of farm labour. This is possible only to a limited extent as the Indian farmer is very wary of uprooting his family from the existing village to a new place. So, the distance he can buy the land from his home has to be not more than a one or two hour commute for him.

Dairy

Dairy farming is another source of income for the farmer. However, the average size of a dairy farm in India is just about two cows or buffaloes. Yes, indeed that is very limited. It's basically a couple of cows in every backyard which doubles up as a dairy farm. Some of the produce is consumed at home but the rest is sold to the nearest milk collection centre. Over the years with the cost of maintaining a cow going up and the milk prices being stable to down, this has not proven to be a very profitable activity. As mentioned in the previous chapter, grazing grasslands used to be free earlier but now have to be paid for. Even so, the milk collection centre adds to the household income and is especially important during times of bad monsoons and this has become a part of the ecosystem in which the Indian farmer thrives. The milk collection centre acts as a funding source of the last resort, if and when the farmer is in need of emergency short-term cash (due to illness or other family emergency). There is rarely any risk of a bad debt here as the borrower is extremely conscious of his social standing and would not want his honour to be compromised. Moreover, the community is small, and a lot of personal facts are known within circles which no one wants to let out.

Renting Out Land — For Farming or Other Uses

Some marginal farmers who did not have the next generation participating in farming have little choice but to consider renting it out. Also, if the patriarch is very old and does not have the fitness levels to toil hard in the farm all day, he may choose to rent out his farmland to other aggregators. Usually such aggregators are not very common as explained in one of the earlier chapters, but where they do exist, farmers do rent out. The usual rule is to receive 50% of the income from the farm for their passive investment and they can sit back and relax. The upside from higher yields or prices goes to the risk taker as he guarantees a fixed amount per acre to the landlord. There is a small percentage of farmers doing this and hence I am not devoting too much space to this aspect, but it is important to note that if aggregation becomes more organised and more people are willing to take the risk, and with younger generations usually not staying back in the farms, this could become a much bigger trend and may not be a bad development after all.

Renting-Out Tractors

Farmers who own slightly larger parcels of land — around seven to ten acres, can afford to own their own tractor to use in the farm. However, they do not need to use it all the time and through the year. So, they have begun renting out their tractors to other smaller farmers. The renting is in the form of the owner operating the tractor for the hirer or just letting the hirer use and run it on its own. Around Rs600 per hour is the additional income that can be made out of this. Assuming three to four hours of renting every day and around three to four months in a year; this adds up to extra income of around Rs240,000 per year; quite attractive even after adjusting for the instalments. There is more reference to this in the following chapter.

The Wealth Effect—The Other Big Driver Of "Earnings"

As for any consumer, what drives spending power is what his earning power is and what the feel-good factor from his wealth effect is. A very similar paradigm exists in the villages too. Almost 100% of rural savings are put into physical assets and valuables; land and gold. This is for long-term investment as well as for productive use and consumption (more land for farming or expanding the house and gold to use during weddings). Hence whenever land and gold prices are going up, the farmer experiences the wealth effect and would spend more. They will use these inflated asset price levels to borrow more (against gold) or sell some of their land (if they get a good offer). A very large part of the rural boom years (from 2009 to 2014) were driven by a mix of these artificial boosters. So, it is tricky to look at the consumption trends and assume the farmer is doing well. This is a trap any government can fall into if they are paying excessive attention to the outcome (demand) and not to the source of the spending power. Maybe this is one of the reasons that the urgency has not been felt to address the farmer problems with long-term solutions, because every time that things start to go bad, due to cyclical and non-agricultural reasons, the farmers' spending power goes up and the government heaves a sigh of relief or feels that the problem has been solved or postponed for now and they can take a breather or provide a patchwork solution.

Perfect Cocktail Turns into a Perfect Storm

Governments usually have seen the farmer as a vote bank and tried to appease them before election years. So, if it's not broken, don't fix it, or fix it with a bandage rather than do a full surgery on the problem area. This point gets further highlighted when the opposite happens. That is, when the wealth effect boosters turn the other way as has happened in the last three to four years. Property prices have fallen a fair bit across the country ranging from 10% to 30% in some cases. The point is driven home strongly because this has had an immediate impact on spending; a correlation more pronounced than one would have expected. It is also a coincidence that along with a waning asset cycle, monsoons played truant and MSP hikes also flatlined and NREGA projects also started dwindling. So, the perfect heady cocktail turned into a perfect storm. This should be deeply understood to avoid a repeat. The other physical asset — gold — also has a complex effect on farmers wealth levels and, hence spending power, because farmers have been used to rising gold prices over the years, they see it as a very long-term investment to be passed on to future generations, especially through the wedding gift channel. Hence when in need of some funds, they would not sell, but borrow against their gold. This is the reason scores of financial services companies have ventured into gold loans for the rural folk.

This supply has made it easier for them to borrow and hence increased demand, (more about this in the credit section). When prices of gold fall and there is a chance of a margin call on the farmer, he would rather repay the loan and get it released then pay up more. So whatever liquidity is available is used up to release the loan. Even in better times, with a round of good monsoons or a good crop and the farmer has some excess liquidity, before he can use it for increasing consumption, he tends to use it to *repay* his gold loans and get the wealth back home. This is the main reason why time and again corporates and forecasters alike have got the rural demand picture wrong. With one or even half a good monsoon, people start expecting an immediate pick-up in rural demand and for rural themed stocks start going up, without realising that the debt levels are such that the first flow of liquidity goes in some balance sheet repair rather than a burst of consumption. This is a quirk of the rural economy, which is not easily observed or understood and this characteristic only makes the dynamics of rural income, wealth and spending power so complex.

Trip Diary #3 — Spending Priorities

On one of our house visits, we were warmly welcomed by the women folk in the house (three of them) while the men (father and son) sat quietly, not very sure what we were going to ask but also surprised that we were addressing the women rather than them. We were offered some local sweets and some tea and once we settled down, I asked the oldest lady in the house what she was saving up for. They all started exchanging glances and after some nudging answered that there are no savings to spend from. Whatever they earn is barely enough to run the house. So, I had to change my question. I asked Gamjibai, the old lady, if there were to be a bumper crop this year, where she would spend the excess income. Pat came the reply — save it for my son's higher education at a private school some distance from home. We were taken aback at the speed and clarity with which she said that. I was expecting maybe a television or a two-wheeler, and I actually asked her why not some of those things. It's then that one of the men pitched in. He said they have long stopped spending money on unproductive things. They already have a two-wheeler and would buy another only if it helped in earning extra money. They rather save and spend on education which will ensure a better life for their children…

CHAPTER 3
Spending Power

It's always of great interest to economists and investors where the rural folk are spending or what their priorities are in the future. Are they going to spend more or save more? If incomes are growing where does the incremental dollar go? Or even if they plan to save more, how are they doing it? Is it in physical assets like gold and property or financial assets like deposits, insurance, shares and bonds? Hence this has been a very important part of what I have tried to gauge all through these trips. To gauge this, it has been very useful to visit dozens of stores and retail outlets across products and services as well as getting into focus group discussions with village households.

One would usually assume that the typical rural consumption basket will see a big boost with improving income or spending power and vice versa. Implying more spending on two-wheelers, tractors, televisions, refrigerators and electric appliances like fans and lights as well as trading up into more branded consumer goods like soaps, shampoos and toothpaste etc. But over time we have found few very interesting insights into the rural spending psyche which has changed over the years.

The link and sequentiality between movements in farm income, allied income, wealth, savings and spending and its timing is intriguing to say the least and hides beneath it a lot of insights and reasons why it is so difficult to gauge the timing and extent of demand or its recovery from the rural economy. One good monsoon does not make a (shopping) season. Corporates have been disappointed time and again by the delayed pick up in rural demand. One of the reasons is that the harm done to the rural balance sheet has been pretty severe given the string of bad monsoons and all the other reasons discussed in the previous chapter — that one good monsoon is not going to make them open their wallets. The first improvement would go to maybe repay some debt and the next would go to increased longer-term productive consumption. Any further improvement would probably go to add to some sort of savings given they have seen the high volatility in their income. Only then, with a more structural improvement in their income and earnings power would they return to increasing consumption expenditure and the trading up syndrome as we have historically known it. Hence there exists a long lag between income improvement and discretionary consumption spending.

Spending on services: Firstly, there is a lot more money spent on services than on goods. Telecom, education and entertainment are three important areas where increasing spending is being diverted. Secondly, a lot of spending is taken away by home improvement (building an extra floor before a wedding or as the family expands) and family weddings. The latter is particularly troublesome as the social fabric and order is such that everyone outspends their means (keeping up with the joneses) and invites practically the whole village.

A) Newer Areas of Spending Focus

A lot more farmers are changing their spending patterns. Rather than spend on just buying the next vehicle they are spending more on appliances, home improvement, telecom, education and jewellery. This has led to national brands expanding rural penetration and distribution. Companies selling fans, coolers, lights and home appliances are seeing promise in reaching out to rural areas. But it is also pretty clear that the next big thing in rural marketing has to be services. Whether it is Financial Services (already happening and discussed at length in the upcoming chapters), health care or education and infotainment, these four areas are going to form the new pillars of the next big consumption boom in the villages. Companies that are trying to make a systematic foray into it nationwide or are already in a position to capitalise on it will be interesting to watch and engage with in further such discussions.

Spending on education: Children's education is taking top priority in the monthly budget. As government schools did not offer a good learning environment due to lack of teachers, inadequate curriculum or sheer parental aspirations, kids started increasingly attending private schools. This costs money. With an average of up to three children per household, it meant almost Rs1000 per month just on tuition. The private schools are usually some distance away from the village. Many villages have a school bus or other shared transportation to ferry the kids to and from the school, and this adds another Rs1000 per month. This has clearly become a big priority of parents and this came out very clearly in almost all my conversations with the farmers and their families, as well as with the other senior village opinion leaders. This has further links with topics on household leverage and education.

B) Smart Telecom Consumer

Several focus group discussions with mobile phone users across villages and age groups showed that almost every household has one or two phones. Half the phones are smart phones and the bulk of the usage on the phones is to watch videos, listen to music, browse sports sites and some news as well. WhatsApp is of course one of the staple uses. This presupposes data access, and hence quality of the footprint and speed are the two most important things. There is a sense that paying Rs100 to 150 a month is seen as something they are getting hooked to and this may mean pricing power may slowly return for the carriers. One of the comments by a user was that if the current difference in speed and network footprint remains, they would not mind paying Rs30 to 50 per month extra to stick with the better-quality network. The shift in market shares of players may be faster and stickier than you think! The good part is that now the villager is limited by only the imagination of the information supplier. Multitudes of apps and information services can be launched to feed the farmer with relevant information about crops, weather, prices, job opportunities, wealth creation opportunities as well as productivity enhancers like aggregation and shared economy. Finally, education and healthcare can take a major turn upwards. I will talk more about the *DigiGaon* in the last section where I highlight the future of rural demographics.

C) Vocational Training

As job opportunities remain a challenge and primary education in villages lacks quality, the rural folk are willing to spend money to get better in English speaking skills. The first things that hit me on my second trip in 2012 was the dozens of hoardings of English speaking training centres that had mushroomed, which marked both sides of the road at least three to five kilometres before I even reached the village. These centres can charge up to Rs5000 for a three-month course promising to make you more confident for job interviews with better command over the language and presentation skills. That is a lot of money and the fact that there are dozens and dozens of these all across the country shows a few interesting observations: a) the employment opportunities are not strong and hence up-skilling is needed, b) schools do not provide good English speaking skills and c) the villagers are willing to spend such high sums to improve the future of their kids. Indeed, this is something that has to be looked at closely. More on education in section four.

Income generating spending: It has been very encouraging to note that despite leading a fairly simple lifestyle which is wanting in many of the comforts that any upwardly mobile household would want to spend on, spending priorities have moved towards more sensible areas like focusing on productive assets rather than purely consumption spending.

Durable goods are bought only if it can be also put to some productive use, like buying a two-wheeler to use for transportation of products like milk for example; buying a tractor to rent out or buying an SUV to start a transportation business, choosing to spend on travel abroad for a family member seeking employment overseas is another example. Even spending over home improvement (asset creation) is a more welcome spending than that on pure consumption. Similarly, farmers have increased the renting in of tractors rather than buying a new one or buying a second-hand tractor instead of a brand new one. Coupled with fragile income growth, this propensity to not do profligate spending may be another reason why overall rural consumption growth has been weaker than most people have expected to see manifest in traditional areas of rural spending. For several years now, corporates who have large rural exposure have expected a pick-up in the near-term (a few quarters ahead) but this has not materialised. The expectations arose from income growth calculations or reportedly good monsoons, but neither translated into any boom.

The Haze of Tractor Demand

Another key area of spending by the farmer is to buy a tractor. However as mentioned above, buying second-hand tractors or renting tractors is becoming an increasing trend among the smaller farmers. On our trips we have spent a disproportionate amount of time on tractor demand, as one of the important ways to play rural consumption for investors has been through companies that sell tractors or finance them. Hence several important insights on tractor demand are worth sharing. Demand for a tractor is driven by multiple things. Agriculture is only one of several drivers: a) Industrial transportation: tractors are not only put to agricultural uses, but industrial applications of transporting goods, is one of the important additional uses, b) Tax arbitrage: using tractors instead of small trucks to save taxes / duties is another. (Duties are higher on commercial vehicles.) c) The construction and mining industries are also very common uses. In fact, it will not be wrong to say that in many parts of the country and during many periods, non-agricultural use is larger than agricultural use. People also ignore the increasing use of second-hand tractors and renting versus buying. Moreover, tractor demand is concentrated disproportionately in certain provinces of the country. When these states experienced either a bad drought, dip in construction activity, or ban on mining activities, tractor demand took quite a beating. d) Financing: tractor companies and financiers incentivised the farmer by allowing low or no down payment. This ease of financing has made even some very small farmers buy tractors with plans to rent them out . Hence this has also been artificially propping up tractor demand, due to supply of credit. As dependence on financing increases, so does the volatility of demand due to the withdrawal of NBFCs (Non-Banking Financial Companies) from the market or if they become more stringent. There has been a phase in 2014 to 2015 period where several finance companies did start withdrawing and it had a visible impact on tractor demand in those areas. In fact we note that underlying demand for replacement is very weak. Although average life is supposed to be eight to ten years, most farmers and even those who rent out their tractors run them for ten to fifteen years and keep repairing them rather than upgrading. If a second tractor is purchased it's really as a second one and not as a replacement. That's why I call the situation 'the haze of tractor demand' as the picture is really not clear.

Lastly, how purchases are financed is interesting as gold or KCC (Kisan Credit Card) loans are used to pay the down payment and in many cases dealers make an 'advance sale' meaning up to six months are provided to even make the down payment, while the buyer can walk away with the tractor on the spot! But more of this on the next section, on leverage in rural India. It has been profitable for financiers to finance tractors as they give a three year loan with a 30 to 40% down payment. After three years, the second-hand value of the tractor is still around 60%. So, it looks like a safe bet provided they can get their hands on the vehicle to repossess. The multi-use of tractors has also affected demand for light commercial vehicles (LCVs) as farmers prefer buying tractors as most of their needs can be met by tractors.

Two-Wheelers

Two-wheelers are one of the main big-ticket item villagers spend on. No surprise that nearly 60% of overall two-wheeler demand is rural. The reasons to buy are quite diverse though. Although 70% of purchases are believed to be for personal use, only 25% are first time buyers which means:
a) the majority of the purchase is for a second vehicle in the house — either for the brother, son or even for the daughter.
b) another big driver of demand is for productive use as mentioned above; particularly milk sellers and other small merchants who sell from door to door or supply small items to retail shops. c) Another very important driver, which is quite quirky, is buying to give as a wedding gift. Some retailers in certain feeder towns have claimed it to be as high as 55% of their demand coming for wedding gifts. This is a long-standing

tradition—the bride's father gifting the groom—in India which is still quite prevalent in small towns and villages.

This also means two-wheeler demand can be quite resilient, as it is for weddings or income generation (milk delivery etc.). Social pressure is something which also drives demand. If a neighbour has bought a two-wheeler, others will feel the pressure and may bring forward a purchase otherwise planned in the future.

Although I will cover this in the chapter on rural leverage, it is pertinent to highlight here that up to 40% of purchases could be financed even in small towns which are feeders to the villages. Hence higher rates or stricter lending norms have an immediate impact on demand which otherwise may not have been felt. This reduces the resilience a bit. This is quite a startling figure prima facie but will all seem very logical once you have gone through a few more chapters. Linkage to the wealth effect as explained above is quite stark, as a 30% fall has been seen in demand in quarters where property prices had started falling. The recent crunch in the financial sector has clearly manifested itself in significant slowdown in demand which is widely known now but was a rich and prescient insight these rural visits gave much ahead of time.

SUVs

Another important part of the shopping basket for the farmer is an SUV. Yes, that is not a typo. SUVs which would otherwise be thought of as an urban phenomenon are actually very strongly entrenched in the rural economy. In fact, SUVs first started selling in India by home-grown brand Mahindra & Mahindra. Its Bolero has been the bestselling utility vehicle in

India. Long before Toyota launched the Qualis, it was Bolero that was ubiquitous on rural Indian roads. This again has to be understood in the context of what applications an SUV is put to. The SUV is seen as a rural means of transportation not for personal use but as a public transportation means. Given the lack of rural public transportation, small entrepreneurs end up buying an SUV and operating it as a public transport vehicle. Given tough rural roads, rugged SUVs have been the vehicles of choice. It is no wonder then that 70% of all Bolero sales have been to rural India, and hence it is also not a surprise that SUV customers are actually tractor customers substituting tractors with SUVs if the application is less industrial. This brings out a very interesting paradigm that in rural India, the boundaries between an LCV, tractor and SUV are all so blurred that demand dynamics also get confusing. This indeed was one of the most interesting revelations of my trips into rural India — understanding tractor demand and how it blurs between its various applications and hence drivers.

Jewellery

We have visited several jewellers in the villages over the years. This remains an important part of the spending — as long-term savings for the daughter's wedding or for consumption. Two main points are worth noting. The habit of the household to stick to the old family jeweller is loosening up for sure, as the younger generation is more focused on better designs and less on old tradition. This was evidenced by several young entrepreneurs from wealthy families started off as franchise partners for national branded jewellers or set up shop from scratch taking on the establishment so to speak. In both these cases, the families had no connection with the jewellery business in the past. The second point which is on the flip side is that over the years many jewellers have opened up shop and there is clear cannibalisation taking place. Plus, a very large part of the business is done on credit although the ticket sizes are very small. This shows two things; one, that new players find it difficult to survive as they don't know the market that well and can't get the credit right and two, that this means the old family jeweller model still works because they are the ones who can take the credit bet. Frankly, trends in demand for jewellery (affordability and credit) and supply (new branded or entrepreneurial entrants and their survival) are not very clear, and this is I think itself an important fact to take on board; that things are a bit in flux and will take some time to settle down.

The Savings Myth

That brings me to the last part of this chapter which is about savings. It may seem a little ironic to discuss savings when it appears the financial conditions of farmers have been quite fragile in the recent past, but it is important to try to understand this as well. Usually villagers do not have any meaningful savings. There is no concept of savings in fact. This points to the fragility of the income stream and the subsistent nature of farming in India.

With the government efforts towards financial inclusion and *aadhar*-linked bank account opening, it has become possible for benefits to be transferred to them directly to their accounts via DBT (Direct Benefit Transfer). This brings them into the formal economy and allows them to slowly climb up the ladder of financial products — from savings accounts to debit cards and fixed deposits and slowly going up to insurance and eventually mutual funds. A fair amount of time has been spent on trying to understand the occurrence of this in villages. The key response we have got is always that there is a lack of savings to deploy it into various optional channels. This gets validated when you are able to do some simple maths around their yearly income and costs given their family size including the fact that whatever they do save they use up for family weddings, house improvements or for supporting children's higher education.

In a bad time, some illness in the family would use any savings up if anything was left. Hence in this context, the government initiative to provide health insurance of up to five hundred thousand rupees per family for all secondary and most tertiary hospitalisation is indeed quite a positive thing. Once this is done and structurally income levels are lifted, savings can start in the true sense of the word and slowly get diverted to financial assets other than cash and deposits. In fact, as we will discuss in length in the next section, the rural household is far from having financial surplus to save and invest; they are currently quite indebted and the leverage is only rising…loans are one financial product on the ladder they have climbed quite fast.

Section 2
Borrowing and Leverage

The Second Trip
Tamil Nadu — villages near Vellore

— This was the first focused trip. Just three guests from Australia, China and India had come with a very specific agenda. So, this was not just a rural immersion but a deep dive of sorts into specific topics. We had to send people a few days ahead to arrange for villagers who are engaged in different types of professions and could answer questions from a first-hand perspective. This was also the first time we did focussed breakout group sessions after the main open house.

Trip Diary #4: Advance Sales, Supermarkets and The Hierarchy of Repayments

Advance Sales

"It's an advance sale," explained Ravish Kumar, the sales manager at a tractor dealership in a small town in rural southern India. I scratched my head to figure out what it could mean and looked at some of my colleague to see if they looked any more enlightened. We had to probe him more to explain. This is a sale where the buyer is taking a loan to purchase a tractor but does not have the ten or fifteen percent of the price to pay as his down payment. The dealership is more than happy to let him "buy" the tractor as there is need to book sales and hence, they allow the farmer to make the "down payment" in instalments. Yes, ironic as it may sound, even the down payment is done in instalments, and hence the sale is called an "advance" sale because he can drive away with the tractor in "advance" of making any payment. That effectively made the tractor 100% financed.

Supermarkets and Loans

This incident in 2015 made me very conscious of the extent to which the rural ecosystem was embedded with credit and loans. In fact, way back in 2012, I met a bank manager in a village and he first hinted to me on how fast the rural loans were growing (20% at the time when overall banking sector was growing loans barely at 10% per year). One of the consultants on rural marketing that I was speaking to for arranging some of these trips, also told me once about this rural supermarket where you could buy agricultural inputs as well as routine household consumption items and use the

Kisan credit card to pay for it. When we walked out of the store, I realised debt is more widespread than one thinks...

The Hierarchy of Loans

Mr Shashi, a loan collection officer at a state-owned bank had just returned from a long day in the field and the last thing he wanted was to bump into a group of strange looking people, asking even stranger questions about things he'd rather not talk about. When he realised there was no way out and we were waiting for him with his boss, he gave up, threw himself down on the rickety chair and ordered himself a cup of very strong, very sweet tea... as if to tell us he needed the energy to face our questions. Once we started shooting out our questions at him, he seemed to enjoy them and took his time to answer. One of the questions was on his experience on borrowing for tractors and default experience on Kisan credit cards. That is when he told us about how there is a hierarchy of loan repayments. The first flush of funds is always used to get the gold back home. "Gold?!" I asked. Yes, farmers routinely pledge their gold to borrow for medical emergencies, a wedding in the family or some home improvement that they want to do. Keeping up with the Jones' is very prevalent out in the county too and each wedding has to be grander than the previous one, hence spending is always on the rise! The second flush of funds would go to repay the private finance companies from where they may have taken a tractor loan and the final flush (if there is so much cashflow) would go to the state-owned banks.

A mix of these interactions made me realise how deep the borrowing culture has become and how high the dependence on loans is.

CHAPTER 4
The Start of the Gravy Train

Leverage in The Rural Household Balance Sheet — Causes and Context

Where do you go when your crop fails, or you get very low prices for your produce, but you still have to spend on that wedding in the family or take care of a medical emergency? You go to the bank to borrow. But what happens if the bank comes to you? You get a very strong habit of borrowing to maintain your lifestyle or needs regardless of your income. Add to this the habitual government tendency to waive farm loans in every election year and this gets even more deeply embedded. Yes indeed, the extent, speed and spread of indebtedness in rural India is one of the most under-appreciated topics in the rural economy.

When at the peak of the cycle the farmer got used to high levels of consumption afforded to him by higher MSP prices and wealth effect, the level of consumption became sticky. When fortunes reversed, with lack of social security (crop or health insurance) or any meaningful savings, the farmer seems to have turned towards the financial system to continue his consumption spree. This explains the conundrum of continued strong consumption by rural India and the increasing growth of financial services companies. Over the years, benign government policies to boost farm credit also led to unfettered borrowing by farmers to even finance their consumption — at least the big-ticket ones like weddings and home improvement. A well-intentioned policy can also cause harm and hence sometimes growth in the economy and has to be taken with a pinch of salt given how much of rural consumption is coming from such loans. Over the years and over the various visits it is startling to see how embedded this habit has become.

There are several causes why this indebtedness has taken root.

But before that it is important to remind ourselves how income and wealth and hence spending power of the farmer has been strongly supported by certain drivers which did not prove to be permanent or structural (high MSP prices, NREGA projects, rising gold and land prices).

So, when with a turn in events income and wealth effects diminished or almost vanished, the farmer was left with a sticky habit—that of higher spend levels than his sustainable income could support, which is what started and accelerated the trend of the use of loans by the farmer. As the perfect storm hit the farmer, the memories of the heady cocktail were difficult to erase and the lower crop prices, bad monsoons and drying up NREGA jobs all put pressure on the farmer and he increasingly turned to debt.

Apart from this change, the rural community also faces routinely sudden short-term needs for funds due to crop failure due to inadequate rains, pest attacks or loss of livestock. The way to solve or cope with this problem is either using personal savings (only about a third of the needs are met by savings) and the rest is solved by borrowing — from a formal or informal sector or from friends and family. Another survey recently showed that almost all rural households had faced one such cash crunch in the last six months.

Government policies to increase credit (KCC) and financial inclusion supported this trend. Deeper penetration by the financial services companies and technology have brought the lender to their doorstep and now actually to their fingertips (with smartphones and *aadhar* linked loans).

Repeated farm loan waivers made it a habit. The extent to which this is now embedded in the routine lifestyle of the villagers is a cause for concern and hence something to socialise and debate. As per some recent national surveys in 2018 at least half of all rural households were indebted.

This deeply embedded habit of borrowing can be verified from another angle too. Over the last decade or so, despite various economic cycles and volatility in the monsoons, rural demand, which is nearly 40% of overall consumption in India, has seemed to not only hold steady but actually has shown growth and buoyancy. People have attributed this to the low base of farmer incomes and hence growth, or to government policies (doles and pricing). However, if one looks deeper at it there have been several periods where none of the tailwinds existed, still rural consumption held up quite strongly and this means other forces have been giving a boost to consumption — namely borrowing.

As recently as the festive season of 2018, there is ample evidence of this dichotomy mentioned above. Another recent visit to some villages in Uttar Pradesh showed that farmers are extremely stressed due to low crop prices and a not-so-even monsoon that year. There were a lot of complaints on how they are struggling to make ends meet. On the other hand, during that time we saw day after day of earnings commentary from companies doing business in rural India, highlighting rural demand as the only bright spot. A leading car maker reported no growth in sales over the previous year but said it was despite a big decline in urban demand, implying at least a 10% growth in rural demand. Another leading maker of bakery items, once reported a low single digit growth in overall volumes but a significantly higher double-digit growth in rural. This dichotomy is now getting common but still remains confusing.

So, the answer to the puzzle clearly seems to be the increasing loans, leverage and indebtedness in the rural household. It may sound strange that when all Indian household debt to GDP is only 9% rural would be even less; and how can that be something to even talk about, leave alone worry about? Agreed that the absolute numbers are and may be low but often it is the pace of increase in loans and not the absolute level that makes a difference. Also, it is the percentage of incremental consumption funded by loans versus income growth that is what we are trying to understand.

Is the farmer taking loans for daily consumption? Is he borrowing against his family jewellery (gold loans were booming a few years ago and may actually have reached saturation)? or is it that their income is actually not under that much stress and the whining is only to get their loans waived? As anything in life, the truth lies somewhere in the middle and there is a bit of both in the mix. Some stress, some posturing and some loans lead to this robust consumption which otherwise would defy logic.

The Shape of You — What Has Shaped the Rural Balance Sheet?

It is worth dwelling a little deeper into some of the reasons highlighted above. How lower crop prices, high dependence on NREGA project, eventual drying up of that pipeline and leakage or delays in project payments have lately played havoc with the farmer's finances.

Low MSP, high NREGA dependence: After many years of very high annual price increases in the MSP (even touching 30 to 40% in some years), the new government since 2014 became focused on controlling inflation and hence reduced the price hikes dramatically, to just about 3 to 4% per annum. This of course also coincided with lower global soft commodity prices and gave a cushion to the government to enable them to push this through. A few years of just 3 to 4% price hikes have squeezed the margins of farmers and their disposable income. The NREGA projects that were started in the early 2000s have been providing a material boost to household income in rural India as described in detail in previous chapters. In the last two to three years however, the overall volume of NREGA projects has come down quite a fair bit and this has also caused pressure on the overall farmer household income. As highlighted earlier, at the peak this was accounting for up to a third of the household income, hence its loss caused a material dent.

Disappearance of land buyers: During the years from 2005 onwards, there was a big investment cycle in India and corporate groups were planning large real estate projects / townships as well as setting up industrial parks and factories. The government was also building industrial zones, roads, bridges and other infrastructure. This meant that there was a bid on the farmers land and into the run up to the global financial crisis in 2008, land prices were soaring. Many farmer families sold their land or part of it and raked in sizeable cash flows. This boosted the wealth of rural households to a very large extent. Even those who did not sell felt rich and enjoyed the feel-good factor. There are so many stories of farmers getting tempted with big offers for their land and selling off, wasting away that newfound liquidity on extravagant consumption but then repenting that they had no income earning asset left when the next down cycle hit them. Once the asset cycle turned and the investment cycle went sour there was no bid for their land. Due to corruption allegations, and difficulty in getting approvals for projects (environment, forest etc.), new investment came to a complete standstill from 2012 onwards. As this collided with the turn in MSP prices from 2014, the farmer faced a negative wealth and negative income effect.

Flat gold prices: Another contributor to the so-called wealth effect was the rising gold prices during the overall asset inflation cycle. As it is very common for rural households to do their primary saving in physical assets; gold basically other than land, with rising gold prices the farmer felt a feel-good factor and wealthy. At the same time rural penetration of gold loan finance companies increased significantly and borrowing against gold for short-term needs became quite easy. This combination added to the overall feeling of prosperity and consumption. When the gold prices also started falling quite hard and then completely flat lined for a very long time, this support line was also gone.

Lower rates: Just as this combination of negatives dented

the income and wealth effect, while the needs had risen of which the farmer had got used to, there was one saving grace. Interest rates in India started dropping as overall growth slowed down and inflation fell. This made borrowing costs cheaper for the household, and as supply and ease of drawdown also increased, the whole gravy train of leverage started moving rapidly into the psyche of the rural households.

Trip Diary # 5: KCC on Steroids

Sushant Kumar repeatedly raised his hand with visible excitement when a question was thrown at the large group of farmers we had assembled as part of our open house. The first question was, 'Who uses a Kisan Credit Card regularly?' and the second one was, 'Who in the room has their passbook with them?'. We wanted to see what this "passbook" looked like and how people used it on a regular basis. Sushant, a slim young man in his thirties, was a second-generation farmer but his elder brother was running the family farm while he was doing, small odd-jobs in the village and nearby towns.

Sushant was eager to show us his KCC. While we all gathered around him (some fifteen of us) he whisked out his wallet to our surprise (we were expecting a large passbook style document) and pulled out a shining new credit card and took us to the nearest ATM machine to show us how he uses it. The card was actually a normal bank debit card called the Rupay card.

He mentioned that he got this smart card recently and it had replaced his old passbook. This now allows him to walk up to any ATM machine and withdraw funds. He uses it a few times a month, even for small ticket consumption purchases including a pack of cigarettes or a bottle of the local spirit... indeed consumer credit had truly reached the villages!

CHAPTER 5
Good Idea, Bad Execution

The Rise and Faults of the Kisan Credit Card

A mechanism to provide cheaper credit to farmers for their working capital and capital expenditure needs — the Kisan credit card (KCC) — became a tool which was misused by the farmer as it was difficult to monitor its end use and led to over-consumption and delayed payments. This chapter tries to pinpoint the scheme structure as the root cause of several of today's embedded problems, as well as how the KCC became a political tool in the hands of the government to use as a quick band aid solution for all farmer ills. Indeed, a good intention executed badly.

Good Intentions, Bad Execution

A glance over the evolution of the KCC shows that this idea was first mooted in 1950 to see how borrowing could be made hassle free for the farmer to get the right quantum of loan quickly. The other important objective was to save the hapless farmer / villager from the usurious ways of the money lender.

We have all grown up watching Bollywood movies depicting the bad and heartless ways of the local money lender who is just waiting for a chance to exploit the borrowers. While not as bad or dramatic, the lender does charge very high rates even if he does help with super-fast "disbursement". Stories of this exploitation are well and widely known and hence one of the main objectives of the government was to rid the farmer of this dependence and provide a legitimate channel of pre-harvest and post-harvest working capital financing.

Close to a dozen committees were set up since 1950 to dwell on the topic of agricultural finance and the last report was published in 1997. After this the KCC scheme was kick-started by NABARD (National Bank for Agriculture and Rural Development) in 1998 and has gone through various modifications. So, a lot of thought has gone into the various issues involved in it, not to take anything away from the rigour of the process and the good intentions at heart but certain aspects are worth noting.

Double the Limit, Half the Size and Then Some...

Of a total base of roughly one hundred and fifty million farmers there are currently approximately seventy-five million active, operational cards. Excluding some dual cards / double counting, there were some 40% of unique farmers (sixty million) who have such credit cards. This penetration has been going up over the years. With every passing few years, the scope of the KCC has been widened. First the limit itself has been increased several times. The limit is supposed to be fixed based on the land holdings and the supply of finance which is basically the estimate of production costs. Up to a loan of

Rs100 000, the farmer does not need to pledge his land ownership papers with the bank. Moreover, until the first Rs300 000 of loan, the farmer can borrow at just 4% per annum versus the 10 to 20% per year he would have to pay elsewhere.

On a rule of thumb basis, initially a loan of up to Rs50 000 was allowed per acre of farmland provided you had a minimum of two acres. This was later revised to Rs100 000 per acre and given to farmers even with one acre of land. In 2019, this has been further increased to Rs160 000. Soon it was also allowed to use a fifth of the limit for personal consumption expenditure. This just had the effect of increasing the lending value of the farmer's asset. A few years back, the government introduced the Smart Rupay Card to replace the passbook-style KCC. Already one in ten KCC cards have now converted to these smart cards and the government is pushing hard to get a much higher penetration. The government push has had the desired effect. Overall utilisation of even the higher limits have gone up to 83%. Already over the years farmers who used to use only part or actually the minimum loan amount they were eligible for, now drawdown the maximum they can. It is cheap funds after all and some of them also on-lend it at higher rates and pocket the difference.

Not only that, once the government allowed consumption expenditure as part of this, even the non-agricultural usage of these loans have gone up. The only aspect that has kept a lid on these loans is that beyond Rs300 000, the discount on the interest rate is removed and hence there is not much incentive for the farmer to borrow. Secondly, due to the need to pledge papers beyond a Rs100 000 loan, large land-owning farmers who do not need much money find it concerning to pledge land for small loan amounts. With these compelling facts, it is no surprise that the KCC accounts for a very large portion of farm credit.

The End Use Problem

As per the government rules for kisan credit cards, the primary objective was to bridge the working capital gap of farmers and prevent them from going to the village money lender who would exploit them in their time of need. It was also meant primarily for working capital to buy seeds, fertilizers, pesticides and irrigation related equipment during the sowing period before they got paid post-harvest. Within this a small portion (one fifth to one tenth) was allowed to be used for personal household expenses. However, over the years this has got turned on its head and a bulk of these loans/credit lines are being used for consumption and non-productive items.

The fact that it has become very easy to "drawdown" these loans through just an ATM card — which can be used in any ATM machine to just withdraw the cash, has only added to the problem. This is another example of "supply of credit" and "ease of use". We were surprised to learn that people use this limit to even buy a twenty-rupee (25 cents) pack of *bidis* — cigarettes made with tobacco wrapped in a leaf.

Speaking to dozens of state-owned bank branch managers over the years has shown that the end use has significantly got diluted and they have no way of monitoring it even if they suspect anything. Everyone knows and everyone turns a blind eye. It is not about just the state-owned banks; it is logistically impossible to keep tabs on the end use. In fact, it is informative to note that the topmost reason for which a farmer borrows money is household expenses and housing related expenses.

I often wonder if it really is so difficult. Why can it not be paid to the vendor directly from whom the farmer buys his requirements? Sure it will increase the paperwork, but then it would have ensured appropriate use of loans and limit the extent of unfettered borrowing. Well, who is complaining as long as you can show solid loan growth? Over the years the misuse has increased, and some bank managers estimate that almost half the farmers taking KCC loans are misusing it for non-productive, personal consumption. This ties up with the survey data I mentioned above. In fact, the loan officers when prodded are so eager to admit and accept that there is a very strong correlation between the extent of misuse and the payment defaults. I had just brought up this topic in a meeting with a loan officer in one of the rural bank branches and I was taken aback at the eagerness with which the officer wanted to share her thoughts on this, as if she has always felt this way and never got the chance to express her concerns — internally or externally. The fact is that hardly 10% of KCC loans involve land paper registration (as others are less than Rs100 000) and only some 1% of defaulters are taken to court for repayment proceedings; nor is there the machinery nor the will to pursue these things and the farmers know it!

Lost cause? While several very recent studies have been carried out by various government and independent bodies like NABARD, ICRIER (Indian Council for Research on International Economic Relations) etc. on the effectiveness and impact of the KCC scheme, our findings from the ground have pointed to the fact that somewhere in the middle phase and in the last seven to eight years the scheme has lost its original focus and cause. Unrestrained borrowing for non-productive end use has gone undetected. More farmers are using more of the limits for more non-productive purposes, but it appears that the scheme was built to go bad.

Built to Go Bad

Who was to foresee that over time, this struggle between demand and supply of loans and the ever-increasing gaps between income and spending, would lead to misuse of a great scheme? But by increasing borrowing limits, allowing personal expenditure, having a light touch on end-use and actually making it so easy to drawdown (ATM card), it looks like the contours of the scheme have now been built to go bad.

The very ease that was desired will probably become one of the biggest negative aspects of the scheme. The fact that now digital and financial inclusion are driving the penetration even deeper, may cause even more abuse and blow so much air into this balloon that a little prick may burst it.

The recent national survey also points out that a material number of limits and loans were approved and given without due process being followed (visiting the farm to assess cropping patterns and hence the production cost and the need for financing etc.). A scheme which was started to protect the farmer from usurious money lenders by offering an easy way to borrow against their land holdings for working capital requirements at low rates, may have turned into the reason for the rapidly rising leverage in the rural household and the bad debts at banks. Unintended consequences of a well-intentioned scheme for sure, but the earlier the government makes it harder to borrow the better…

Farm Loan Waivers and The Moral Hazard

Where the KCC scheme brought the credit culture to the farmer and the progressive easing of norms embedded that in the farmers, the processes made it easy to misuse it — farm loan waivers spoilt the credit culture to a very large extent.

It is intuitive that if due to political or other reasons farmer loans are waived even once, it is natural that going forward new loans will be taken with much lower intentions (if at all) of repaying them. So, while the KCC has been in force over the last two-three decades, there have been at least two to three cycles of waivers across states and this has led to more borrowing with gay abandon. It is very difficult to gauge this behaviour and actions speak louder than words—no amount of questioning will draw forth the truth. It is only cold statistics that lay bare the truth. Innumerable discussions with bank loan officers in rural bank branches have shown the amount of NPLs, slippages and write-offs they take every year on these loans. During election years, drawdowns actually increase as it is only logical to expect a waiver by the government. In fact, bank managers have specifically told us that a few years ago in 2015, the average default rate used to be around 20%. This then jumped to 60% of loan accounts seeing delayed payment after a round of waivers. The key reason they are unable to pay is because they are using it for unproductive purposes or for consumption. On the flip side, when this topic is brought up with the farmers, it becomes a very sensitive issue. In fact, one meets two kinds of farmers. One that believes that they deserve the waiver and have no qualms in missing payments. They believe that during election season (local and central) politicians will offer such sops and they should enjoy the benefits. And the other who appear very conscientious and feel that if they default on a loan, they will not be able to get loans in the future and hence they don't see how they would benefit from not repaying one loan, as they will need to take more and larger loans going forward. They see waivers as something only to benefit the real needy ones who have had severe crop damage due to pest or bad weather and when we speak to this group of needy farmers, they say that the waiver is not as all-encompassing as it may sound in the media when the headline figures are announced (Rs200 to 500 billion). It is actually very selectively applied, and eligibility norms render most of the losses uncovered. Even when they are eligible, the paperwork and red tape is so large, and finally after all this the disbursements take even longer to go through. So actually, when analysing the impact of farm loan waivers, it is very tricky and crucial to understand who is really benefitting from it. A large section of the farming community has not borrowed in the first place so they have nothing to gain. A second section is of compulsive defaulters who are not going to repay anyway. So, it is only a small portion of large farmers who have substantial loans who get this benefit.

Which brings us to the second aspect—the moral hazard. As mentioned above almost in every visit and interaction with farmers we have tried to validate the relatively strong demand data emerging from companies selling to rural India; and in every visit we have come back feeling that if it exists, the demand is not sustainable because the farmer is in bad shape. Every time, the farmers have pointed out their stress due to bad monsoon, pest attacks, low prices, intermediaries exploiting them etc. Over the years it has become also quite clear that there is some element of posturing in this, in the hope of getting a farm loan waiver. In a country where the rural vote bank can cause major swings to electoral outcomes, no politician can really, after a point, ignore such requests, while others may actually promise waivers to get votes as a last resort. In the recent past we have seen even the most well-intentioned administration resorting to such tactics in certain states. In fact, just in the last one year a total of Rs1.3 trillion of farm loans have been waived in states like UP, Maharashtra, MP, Rajasthan etc.

Going forward despite the fiscal implications, it looks like FLWs (farm loan waivers) have become even more mainstream. Every political party (ruling, opposition and regional) are offering it blatantly. It is open season for the farmers. It just goes to show that governments are having to show impact in a very short period of time and as reforms take time, the only way to show something (and get elected or re-elected) is to waive their existing loans.

Trip Diary #6: Finance Row

It was another hot summer afternoon in May, and we were walking the streets of a small feeder town in rural Madhya Pradesh, just a couple of hours drive from Indore—the commercial hub of MP. Our consultant had arranged four to five meetings with various micro finance and small finance banks as well as visits to the branches of a few non-bank finance companies. I wondered how we would manage to cover three to five meetings in the two hours that we had. Well, I realised in a short while, why he was pretty cool about it. In fact, it dawned upon me the moment he said, "We can leave our car here and just walk about to the next few meetings." Yes, they were all very close by but to my real surprise, they were not even close by, they were all located on the same street! Finance Row as it were. We literally went door to door, one "shop" after the other and met four companies in all. They were all financiers across the spectrum of the system. From extremely local micro finance companies, to regional small finance banks, to well established NBFCs, to national private sector top tier banks. Yes, they were all there on that one street hawking their loans to the rural folks armed with their tablets and access to the bureaus database. I marvelled at this financial "all you can eat" supermarket and what it means for the future...

CHAPTER 6
Supply Creates Its Own Demand — Easy Credit, Sticky Behaviour

In pursuit of growth, banks (both private sector and public sector) as well as financial services companies reached the final frontier — read rural India and engulfed, overwhelmed the poor folk with easy-to-take loans whether it is to buy a tractor or build that extra room in their house. Lenders were falling so much over each other that there was someone willing even to finance the down-payment the farmer needed for another loan! This chapter explores the sticky nature of this habit and why the cycle has to be broken sooner rather than later. In fact, the NABARD NAFIS (India Financial Inclusion Survey) 2018 survey throws up very interesting data on this. While the all India indebtedness in rural households was 47%, it was 60 to 80% in the southern states of Andhra Pradesh, Telangana, Karnataka and Tamil Nadu. This is a very high divergence from the average and actually the average ex of these 3 to 4 states would probably be in the low 30% range.

Supply and Demand for Credit

It is easy to understand the demand for credit due to income stagnation and rising consumption needs but when at the same time supply of credit has also jumped up, it can create a lethal combo. That is what has happened; where there was not only a government top down push (KCC and financial inclusion), which was followed through by PSU banks but also private sector financial services companies in seek of growth have bombarded the farmer with easy to take loans. It was open season to win market share as the PSU banks were slow in their processes and from time to time had their stops and starts too. To top it all, the Reserve Bank of India (India's central bank) focused on financial inclusion too (access to banking for all) and hence gave out new small finance bank licenses which had a very high rural rollout obligation. This led to the opening of a lot of branches of all sorts of financial firms in the feeder towns of rural India. Technology has played its role too. With many a bank tying up with local *kirana* stores in villages to act as banking correspondents, the task of actually drawing down loans or repaying the instalments became easier too.

We discussed the KCC phenomenon above and in this part, we will dwell more into the private sector push into rural India and supply emanating from there.

The Banks

Historically the private sector banks have been growing rapidly by expanding their branch network in urban India and deploying aggressive customer service, better technology and user interface to win market share from the public sector banks. But when the pie stopped growing it became difficult to deliver scorching growth with that strategy alone. Hence, they started looking at the next or the final frontier — the untapped rural markets. The PSU banks were wary of lending to the farmers as they'd had a bad experience in the past and also did not have the resources to do proper due diligence, monitoring or recovery. The private sector banks entered this space in the 2000 to 2010 time-frame and started offering loan products for pre and post harvesting needs. They also added products like gold loans and to some extent home improvement and vehicle loans as well. Though initially their agenda was to collect deposits from these new areas, the asset side of things also started coming into focus.

Rural Deluge by NBFCs

The NBFCs in India were always present in rural areas to finance two and four wheelers and also to finance new and used trucks and tractors. These companies also went deeper in search of growth and started offering rural home loans as well as other loan products to the rural folk. As per the latest RBI data, there are a total of some eleven thousand registered NBFCs in India with a total loan book of around Rs22 trillion (approximately $300 billion). Of this the so-called rural exposure (financing of rural homes, home improvement construction loans, tractors, two-wheelers, cars, utility vehicles and gold loans) while difficult to estimate, would be around 20% to 30% ($60 to 90 billion). This has been growing at a rapid clip of approximately 20% to 30% (>100% pa on low base for some) for the last seven to ten years.

Micro Finance and Small Finance Banks

With RBI giving new licenses there opened up a few dozen micro finance companies and small finance banks. All of these had a key strategic focus only on rural areas. They raised funds on a wholesale basis (at 12% to 14%) and lent it out to the rural folk at 18% to 24%. Most of their loans were supposed to be for income generating purposes (self-help groups and joint lending groups) but this has lately morphed into more plain vanilla loans against assets. The presence and penetration of MFI / SFB (Micro Finance Institutions / Small Finance Banks) mushroomed and blossomed in the south and that clearly explains my theory of supply creating its own demand. The reason for this movement to have started from the south could be the generally higher level of literacy or the lower acreage ownership of land in these parts, as well as the fact that over the last five to seven years the southern states have faced more droughts than any other part of the country. The NAFIS study also shows that 20% of households had an MFI relationship (SHG (Self Help Group)) and 65% of all households borrowed money from them for personal needs rather than productive use.

The still active local money lender: In all this we should not forget the friendly neighbourhood money lender. He is still alive and kicking though demonetisation caused a short-term speed bump. My meetings with farmers who still borrow from the money lender show that it is still useful to some who may not be eligible for KCC loans or who may feel that the "friendly" neighbourhood money lender is actually an easier way to get the needed loan quantum even if at a slightly higher rate. Equally my multiple meetings with operating money lenders across states shows that they strongly feel they have a big and real value to add to the system. They help when the farmer has no other avenues to borrow from the system. This flow of loans is always the easiest and fastest to raise and hence adds to the loan supply. In fact, it also shows that a very large portion of farmers or the landless farm worker has almost no other place to turn to.

Ease of Use — The Final Straw

Quantity of supply of credit is one thing and its ease of access / hassle-free access is another important aspect. You may have five companies willing to lend to you but if the process is cumbersome and involving lots of paperwork, it acts as a deterrent. This has also changed dramatically with very quick processing with the minimum of documentation required (the document-light loans), and super-fast approvals. In fact, the joke on "Finance Row" was exactly that; after bargaining for the maximum quantity and best rate, now the borrowers are bargaining for the fastest approval!

This aspect is one of the most under-appreciated parts of the change in the system that needs to be understood well. It is just ironic that given the financial inclusion and digital thrust of the government (a well-meaning drive) it is going to only add to the problem of plenty (of credit), as it comes with very little process, paperwork and strings attached. So, it would not be regressive to add some old school analogue processes even while we progress towards more universal and easy availability of finance. In fact, an expert who focuses on assessment of government schemes had exactly this to say, that, lack of human infrastructure is going to be the biggest cause of failure of various schemes of the government. No surprise then that the highest authorities in the government are now all beginning to talk about administrative reforms—the first time I have heard of this in a long, long time.

This links up with the very first topic we focused on ... income growth of the farmer community. High and easy supply of financing when incomes are struggling is even less desirable and hence the progress of financial inclusion needs to be calibrated along with growth in income too. One cannot speed ahead with the other sputtering and coming to a standstill, as it will only lead to a significant drop in debt service coverage ratios at the village household level. Aggregate data will take years to highlight this to economists and even policy makers and hence the risk we run is it gets too big to resolve, before it gets caught.

The Flip Side of The JAM (Jan Dhan-Aadhaar-Mobile) Trinity

As mentioned above, the entire JAM trinity (universal bank accounts, easy KYC (Know Your Customer) process and the smartphone revolution) and the digitisation and financial inclusion agenda of the government is a double-edged sword. Take for example the fact that only 12% of all KCC cards are currently in smart card format. The reason it is low is because of low density of ATM machines in villages. As this goes up and the government pushes for more smart cards, the drawdown of the KCC loan becomes so much easier that this gravy train may only accelerate from here as the ease of use syndrome will increase the non-productive end use of KCC loans.

The "Lethal Troika" — Waivers, Lending Value and Cash in The Bank

I want to end this chapter with a little powerful message. I call it the "lethal troika". Higher lending value on the farmer's land (KCC limits) allows him to borrow more if he wants or needs funds for large ticket expenses, on the other hand incessant and ubiquitous farm loan waivers encourage the farmer to use that higher limit with little worry and maybe even for some not so important smaller expenses and lastly, the government (state and centre) throw in cash hand outs in the form of monthly income support to take care of the petty expenses (at least NREGA needed you to work)—what a "lethal troika". It is bound to boost consumption (from staples to discretionary spending) and give a false sense of prosperity to the farmer and the government until this all comes back to bite—maybe not as soon as some sceptics think but definitely sooner than the optimists would imagine!

Section 3
Market Structure and The Supply Chain

In the first section on income and earnings we discussed the minimum support price in some detail as one of the income drivers. We also briefly discussed the distribution infrastructure namely the marketplace and the related storage requirements. Since we have spent a lot of time visiting these parts of the rural economy given its importance, it is important to understand this in more depth.

Once the farmer has decided what to grow and using best practices has got a good yield, the story is not yet over. In fact, in many ways, it has just begun. The farmers have to sell their produce at a good price at the right place and time. Yes, these two are important as we are dealing with perishables here. Hence, the two key pillars of the farm economy are the marketplace where the farmer sells his produce and what market price he gets for it. The second and linked topic is that of rural infrastructure for storage of his produce, if he wishes to postpone the sale waiting for a better price. The MSP is a regulated procurement price of the government hence we discussed that in the previous section on income, but here we will focus on the market prices that a farmer is supposed to get for his entire produce on a sustainable basis. Again, the MSPs as mentioned earlier have been really applicable only to two crops so are of limited importance in the larger scheme of things. But these two are so closely intertwined that it is difficult to talk about one without again touching upon the other. So, at the cost of some repetition I have brought the MSP into this section's discussions as well.

It is very interesting to understand what the various systems are and process the government has for procurement, distribution and storage (APMC, FCI, PDS (Public Distribution System), e-NAM (National Agriculture Market) and MSP) and how well they work currently. Admittedly it is a veritable alphabet soup for the layman, and we try to decipher and simplify it here so we can all appreciate what is going on here.

There is hope, with some of the government's intentions to ensure the farmer gets a fairer price without losing too much to the trader. A good monsoon and a good crop can still not ensure the farmer gets a fair price if this value chain is not fixed through APMC reform and better warehousing infrastructure availability. Promises to pay the farmer the difference between the MSP and the mandi price may again be a populist rhetoric rather than the right sustainable solution.

The Third Trip – Haryana – Panipat-Lalheri, Karnal – Chatera and Rajasthan – Bharatpur - Kumher

This was one of my most comprehensive trips with the largest number of participants (seven guests), as well as the longest, spanning four days; and the participants were interested in different sectors rather than all being there to get a general sense. This trip took us deep into Rajasthan (Bharatpur and Kumher) and Haryana (Panipat, Karnal, Lalheri, Chatera). The fact that this was in the cool winter month of November, made it all the more enjoyable to plan and execute. By now the structure had evolved into a science: village walk, open house, feeder town and introducing the "track" during the second half of the day which was spent in a feeder town.

Trip Diary 7: The Friction Is Fictitious

"We are all friends and have been working together for years. All this friction between us *adatiyas* and the farmers is fictitious, and we exist in total harmony." That was Rajkumar Tukaram, the head of one of the storied broker agents of a large APMC *mandi,* trying to brush over the allegations of how *adatiyas* are exploiting the poor farmer in terms of procurement prices. He went on to say that there are lots of vested interests at work who want the public at large to believe that agents are the bad guys in this whole value chain. We were taken aback by this frank and firm outburst from this seemingly short, low-profile old gentleman, who had just welcomed our group of a dozen people with hot local tea and insisted we sweeten it with jaggery instead of refined sugar.

We had reached this meeting a good one and a half hours late but this crowd of some six agents was waiting patiently for us — as if waiting for a chance to redeem themselves. There was also a much larger crowd of farmers gathered outside (at least a dozen) curious to know what we wanted to ask them and more importantly how we could help them. After spending a few hours, it was clear that beneath the calm and camaraderie between the agents and the farmers, there were a lot more layers to peel, to get to the heart of the issues and views of various stakeholders.

CHAPTER 7
Understanding the System and Solutions

The farmer has two ways of selling his produce: to the government at the minimum support price or in the *mandi* at market determined prices. The former is less relevant because historically it has only catered to the kharif crop and only to two crops out of the twenty-three in the basket, although those two (wheat and paddy) account for a very large portion of food grain production of the country. We will focus on the latter here, namely the mandi system. But before we jump deep into that, we should understand the basics of the distribution infrastructure.

The first piece to understand is the government storage. The government runs a storage network of warehouses owned and managed by the FCI. The government runs a distribution network called the PDS through which it supplies subsidised food to the poor people through the ration shops. The government procures food for the PDS and stores it with the FCI. To fix reasonable procurement prices for the farmer it sets up an MSP. Understanding this alphabet soup of MSP, FCI, PDS etc. is crucial to understand what is wrong in the current market structure for agricultural produce and where the change is needed.

The second piece of the puzzle is the MSP. The MSP was introduced in the '70s to prevent exploitation of the farmer and to ensure a minimum price for his produce when the market prices are low due to oversupply or lack of demand. The objective was never to procure unlimited quantity at that price but to act as a back stop and nudge / guide market prices to be in a narrow range around this price. The concept and mechanism of MSP appears to be a very elegant and well intentioned one. (Notwithstanding the point we made in Chapter 1 about it distorting the farmer's choice.) But it was never really tested in its entirety where prices are so low across the board that the government actually has to become that buyer of last resort and put its money where its mouth is. This is what has happened recently and hence it is being put to its test now. Hence what historically was just limited to wheat and paddy now had to be expanded to more crops. The government recently announced a 22% hike in the MSP for example and expanded the list of eligible crops from two, to almost the entire twenty-three which had MSPs. But to buy so much the government needs three things: a) the financial resources, b) the transport infrastructure to procure and c) the storage infrastructure to store all the purchased produce. All these are and have been constraints. However, the government has admitted that if it is not able to procure all of them, it will provide other mechanisms to make good the farmer; and that has indeed been the case and they have then discussed mechanisms for paying the difference to the farmer if they cannot physically procure, which also is fraught with risks. This has brought into focus even more the whole issue of storage and creating a more robust natural marketplace to reduce the farmer reliance on MSPs. For example, the government procures almost a third of the entire country's wheat and rice production through the MSP system. But for all other crops and fruits and vegetables, the government hardly plays any role.

The third piece of the puzzle is the APMC and its mandi system. It is important to understand how this works. Currently there are about eight thousand mandis and sub-mandis all over the country and twenty-two thousand rural *haats* (*Graams* — grameen agricultural markets). The farmer has the option currently of selling at the main mandi, or the sub mandi or go to the rural *haat* (rural periodic markets) and lastly to give it at the farm gate to an aggregator. The government is trying to put the Mandis on to the e-NAM and connect the Graams to the APMC network after upgrading their basic infrastructure to that of a mandi (at a cost of $300 million over two to three years (storage, sheds etc.). All these are the right intentions but will take time. For example, of the twenty-two thousand rural *haats*, only some two thousand have been found viable to bring them up anywhere near the standards of a marketplace. This will reduce the intermediaries in the value chain and bring transparency and better pricing for the farmer. The current APMC mandis suffer from various short comings which we will probe into further below.

Trip Diary # 8: The Mandi System and The Long and Bumpy Road

Late morning one February, we were a small group of only three investors and two of my colleagues. We were travelling in two cars in the interiors of Uttar Pradesh, in search of getting to the heart of the logistics supply chain by going and visiting the two-decade old pioneering initiative by ITC — an e-Choupal. It was supposed to have plugged all that is wrong with the current APMC and mandi eco-system. What better than that, to get a good sense of the issue at hand? Little did we know what was in store for us. My consultant had worked out a short cut route for us to reach this next village. He knew it was going to be a bumpy ride for a short part of this route, which we felt was manageable.

Well, it was not. Firstly, it was not a short ride; it was easily an hour and a half long. Secondly, it was not just bumpy, it was like driving on constant rumble strips for that ninety-minute journey. It was the most horrible road I have ever driven on. I must have decided at least five times on the way that we would abandon this next meeting and head back. But our backs and necks had invested so much on this little adventure that it felt unfair to turn back with each passing kilometre.

My consultant and my colleagues and I could not stop apologising to our guests (Korean and Japanese) and insisted we stop, but our guests were so sporting about it that they wanted to continue. They did in their own polite way mention that the road was a little bumpier than they had expected!

Thank god, when we reached the e-Choupal we were greeted by some very senior people from the company and were taken on a very detailed tour of the site with a very informative demo and explanation. That, and the sweet yoghurt drink (lassi) served after that, made it all worth it.

CHAPTER 8
What You Sell Is What You Get. The Farmer, a Hostage of the Mandi System

Currently the farmer has to sell his produce only at one designated *mandi.* If the mandi is far and crops get damaged on the way, it's his loss. If the mandi agents do not grade his crop properly and offer him an unfair price he cannot do much as he cannot take his produce elsewhere nor can he take it back and hence has to dump it at whatever price he is being offered. The farmer cannot sell his produce directly to the institutional buyer and has to sell it through a registered agent at the mandi. Many of these rules were made to protect the farmer from exploitation but with change in farm dynamics, the purpose is not being served and hence the rules need to change. One of the easiest ways to increase a farmer's income is not to raise prices or reduce costs, but just to give him more of his own value chain and reduce the middleman's share. Clearly that's easier said than done.

Hence on all the rural trips and visits, exploring and understanding the dynamics that drive the mandis was a key objective and hence we spent disproportionate time at such mandis on all our trips. In fact, we visited multiple mandis on each trip, trying to visit one *mandi* per district to meet as many agents and farmers as possible. Admittedly the media had written a lot about the need for APMC reform and how the middleman is the bad guy; that it became even more important to really get to the heart of the matter and hear it from the horse's mouth to understand the actual truth.

The "Middle Story" Of the Food Chain

One of the most important parts of the farmer economy after the produce is ready, is the ability of the farmer to sell it and sell it at a fair price (reflecting costs, product quality, demand and supply). The farmer is the weakest link in this chain and has low bargaining power as the buyer is more organised. The government has a few mechanisms to support the smooth and efficient execution of the entire supply chain. The most important of all is the mandi run by the APMC, which is the official market where the farmer is supposed to bring his produce and the buyers bid for the produce. Price realisation is supposed to be market-driven and based on the quality of the produce.

The APMC is a well-conceived mechanism created in the '70s to help the farmer in selling his produce in a fair manner without being exploited. Thus, several rules were built around this system which may have well served their purpose today. Just a few points to introduce the concept here.

Historically a *mandi* was set up for each agricultural area (comprising of a few dozen villages) so that all farmers could conveniently bring their produce to it and sell it. Farmers from other villages were not allowed to sell into that *mandi*. There were two kinds of mandis. One of grains and crops and one for perishables like fruits and vegetables. Also, the farmer was not allowed to sell directly to the end buyer. Both the seller and the buyer had to go through the agent. Each state government under the ministry of rural development or agriculture set up these mandis. Agents had to register themselves with this mandi to be able to trade in it. Since this is a state subject, it is up to the state government to even have an APMC and then to govern and run it the way it wants. This has led to huge disparities between mandi operations and rules, as well the fact that some states yet do not even have an APMC system. The intra state sale of farm produce is a state subject and hence states have to enact the act. Each state is divided into various market areas and one mandi is set up per market area. The farmer can only sell his produce in that market. Several markets are governed by one committee and all the committees are governed by an agricultural board. Each APMC has representation from farmers, traders and warehouse owners and the board has representatives of each APMC and the relevant government ministry. Except Jammu and Kashmir, Kerala and some union territories, all states have an act enacted. There are about two thousand five hundred main APMC markets across the country and about five thousand sub-market yards. For example, Maharashtra has around three hundred mandis of which about two hundred are active. There are separate markets for perishables (fruits and vegetables); some states have kept fruits and vegetables outside the APMC scope due to differences and peculiarities. The farmer has to sell his produce only through the market, and only a registered licences trader of the APMC can buy. A food processing company or wholesale or retail trader cannot buy directly at the APMC. Hence in many ways the farmer is hostage to the traders as he has to make his first sale only there.

With time, and as the agricultural economy has evolved, there are several issues that have cropped up that need to be addressed.

1) In the current system the farmer does not have access to the end user and has to sell to an agent. The reason this rule exists is to prevent the large end user from exploiting the farmer in a bilateral transaction, hence an auction process via an agent was set up. But the way the auction and agent system has got troubled with corruption and exploitation, the farmer may be better off left to his own devices. Hence direct customer access has again become a key requirement.

2) Farmers prefer to not have any borders and be able to sell across mandis where they get the best price. Currently there is a mandi at every twelve kilometres on average, and there is one for about two hundred to two hundred and fifty villages. Only farmers from those two hundred and fifty villages can access a particular mandi. Even if the prices are better off in a nearby mandi, they are not allowed to access it. At one of the mandis we visited, the farmers mentioned that in a particular year, there was huge over supply in their mandi but drought-like conditions in neighbouring states. Some farmers tried to go and sell there but were stopped from doing it. An open access system is required to share information with the farmer and allow him to sell wherever he wants.

3) Even if they sell at the designated mandi, the agents are not very transparent in the pricing based on the grade of the crop. Grading processes are not very transparent and scientific and the risk of the farmer getting short-changed is high. Farmers often have told us that their produce is not graded properly, and hence auction bids do not reflect the quality of

119

their produce. Grading infrastructure and supervision of this is critical at each mandi, but rarely happens. The whole thing is done in a very casual and ad hoc manner and it appears the agents take advantage of old trust and relationship with the farmer. The trusting farmer does not make a big fuss about it as well. This fluidity will remain until this physical mandi system exists. The earlier it is put into an electronic marketplace, the better.

4) Even the payment cycle for the sale is not well defined and the farmer may get his money after quite a wait. Usually the mandi payment cycle is two to four weeks. Rarely can the farmer wait so long so he agrees to take a discounted price to get immediate cash. The official payment cycle has to shrink given the very fragile working capital cycle the farmer follows. He hardly has any flexibility. A few weeks' delay can upset all his calculations in a very big way.

5) Another troubling issue is the fact that the total twenty-five hundred odd mandis are just not enough (one per two hundred and fifty villages) as they are spread quite far apart and this means a lot of travel for the farmer to sell his produce. In fact, a third of these are not even functioning. Some studies have shown that the farmer needs to travel for an average of twelve kilometres to reach the nearest mandi! This should not be more than five kilometres as per the national farmer commission. This long distance is the biggest problem. It increases the cost of transportation for the farmer and also causes more damage on the way. He loses an entire day to this trip and if prices are not to his liking, he has almost no ability to refuse and try another day. He has to sell and come back. This also forces him to sometimes consider weaker options of selling at the local seasonal markets (rural haats) at lower

prices or worst case just give it at the farm gate to some local aggregator at even lower prices. In all these options, the farmer loses his price. The final yield is way below what he should be getting.

This issue is even negative from the perspective of the buyer—say, a food products company or wholesale or retail distributor needs to buy produce from the farmers. As explained in the first section of this book, corporate or contract farming is not allowed in India in a proper way. Hence to ensure quality of produce, buyers have gotten into various informal arrangements with farmers in areas that they want to buy from.

Currently large food processing companies work very closely with their "contract" farmers in terms of education, use of right farming practices, chemicals, seeds etc. but actually have no right on the produce and have to navigate the APMC *adatiyas* or actually "tag" their produce to make sure their representatives can identify "their" produce and bid for it and secure it. It's quite an inefficient system and ironically something that was supposed to be for the farmer's benefit and to prevent his exploitation, has actually become the source of their exploitation

There have been some efforts by the government to allow more direct access to farmers. The central government passed a model act in 2003 for all the states to follow. The key points of the model act were to allow contract farming and allow farmer to sell to retail users directly as well as to allow any private player to set up a competing market. Also, to not allow the agent to charge commissions from the farmer. It made grading more transparent and the payment cycle completely electronic without chance of manipulation. Karnataka was the only state which really adopted this model act and took it forward. Unfortunately, another good idea has not been adopted across the country as there remains a lot of vested interests. In January of 2013 a revised and updated model act was released.

Recently in 2014, the government took a further step of having one national electronic market to unify prices and make price discovery more efficient. An electronic national market (e-NAM) was proposed to bring fair and transparent market access to the farmer and better prices by removing the middleman. As mentioned at the very beginning of this chapter, the affected parties (namely the agents) have been opposing it tooth and nail and have not allowed it to really pass or progress.

Key Points of the e-NAM System

Currently around five hundred mandis are online and close to four million farmers are using it. It allows the farmer to sell directly to the buyer and get full transparency in the pricing and payment process. Payments can be received online and via the unified payment interface. There are some ninety commodities on this platform already. Buyers can access mandis across the country and compare prices and even traders can do inter-market trade, but currently the bulk of the volume is only intra-market. Only now after the first two years of implementation of this initiative, seven states are trying to start a true inter-state trading platform. This will truly open up the whole nation to the farmer and he can sell his produce at the highest price bid on the system. He also gets paid instantly versus the one- or two-weeks minimum credit period he has to give to the APMC agent. These do address a lot of issues currently faced by the farmers but the fact that less than three percent of the farmers are on it again means there is need for more awareness and also for fixing or ironing out some teething issues with eNAM. It also means all is not broken with the current APMC and adatiya arrangement particularly for the smaller farmers (which make up nearly one hundred and twenty million of the one hundred and fifty million farmers in India).

The Other Side of The Coin — What the Adatiya Has to Say

The *adatiya* — middleman — is often made out to be the bad guy in this whole story. The government and the media have broadcasted this view repeatedly. Our visits have really allowed us to understand his point of view and actually speak to both parties openly to understand the true picture, and clearly, it's not all bad news. The agent historically has played a multifarious role for the farmer which has to be appreciated too. The big accusation on how the intermediaries rip off the farmer is actually not fully true. These are a few things to keep in mind.

Firstly, in all our interactions with the agents and farmers as a group, the farmers seemed to be on very good terms with the agents. The relationship between a farmer and the agent is one of a long-term nature sometime spanning generations and they are not seen on a purely commercial basis. Secondly, in most cases it appears there is a lot of trust between these two parties and trust that has been built over years. If you expect to bring up the word *"adatiya"* and see the farmer fuming—

well no such thing happens. They are all in a pretty cordial and symbiotic relationship. Thirdly, these agents act as informal lenders of the last resort for the farmer too. During times of extreme cash crunch, a really bad crop or a family emergency, the farmer often comes to this very same agent asking for short-term loans, and they are there to help. There is some merit in this ecosystem which if completely removed would harm the farmers somewhat, as well as then they would be at the mercy of the institutional buyers who are not going to extend such informal credit. Lastly, the agents insist that there is nothing amiss between them and the farmers and this whole blame game and mudslinging is done by politicians for their own agenda. They also point to the negatives of the e-NAM system as the payments were initially being delayed for the farmers due to account name matching issues etc.

Private Play

Some large private companies involved in the food processing business have also made some very ground breaking and interesting initiatives. One such company, ITC — set up electronic marketplaces across three or four states and called it e-Choupal. This was started some twenty years ago and primarily to secure its supply of good quality agricultural crops that it needed for its products. We visited one such e-Choupal and were quite impressed with what ITC had put together. It was basically a small two-storey hut which had a computer connected to their network. The choupal provided some basic services which included weighing the produce properly and not charging the farmer for loading or unloading his goods. He ended up receiving 3% to 4% higher prices than at the mandi.

He also received his payment immediately rather than having to wait for one month at the mandi. The model was good but remained restricted to three to four states from where ITC needed to procure its key ingredients. It also was not scalable though, for various reasons including lack of connectivity and continuous power supply. There was a phase when ITC slowed down on this. Initially there was a lot of excitement within and outside ITC about this platform and it was lauded as a very promising future for farm logistics. But sadly, it has not achieved that scale and widespread penetration. Lately it seems to have revived this with e-Choupal version 4.0 and is now targeting ten million farmers by 2022 versus four million farmers currently. Discussions with some e-Choupal staff as well as *sanchalaks* shows that the primary reason for the stunted growth and failure of the format was the lack of reform in the APMC act. When states would not enact the model APMC act of 2003 or 2013, procuring directly from farmers was inherently not possible. This appears to be slowly moving ahead and so is ITC now with its version 4. We have dwelt a bit more on this in the last chapter on technology in agriculture as well.

A Store of Value — Storage and Efficient Working Capital Financing

The second piece of the puzzle is the storage. The storage infrastructure plays into this equation in two ways. One, is storage for the government procurement which it does at the MSP and then distributes it through the PDS system to the poor. Two, is for the farmer, who can store his goods if the pricing is not right at the prevalent market price. As these two affect the farmer in different ways, we will deal with them separately. Better and adequate storage for the government will help the government procure more from the farmer at the stated MSP. Hence making the MSP promise more real. Firstly, let's look at the adequacy of this storage. The current storage infrastructure is run by the government entity called the FCI. The existing government FCI-owned warehouses are old and dilapidated and often open to air with rampant pilferage and loss due to weather and pests and anyway, are only used by the buyer—that is, the government. They own and operate warehouses and godowns across the country. There are two types of such facilities. Open air and covered shelters. The total capacity is 84 million tonnes and given the total grain production of the country is 230-240 million tonnes, it is already inadequate. Plus, it is already storing older produce so spare capacity is limited.

Currently around 70% of this is already utilised. The incremental requirement of storage is around fifty-five to sixty million tonnes hence the capacity shortfall is quite clear. Add to this, other grains and some fruits and vegetables too, as well as the storage needs of the private sector—on a nationwide basis there is definite shortage of space. In fact, the erstwhile planning commission a few years ago had estimated the shortage at thirty-five million tonnes.

The problem also is that many of them are uncovered and lead to a lot of pilferage or damage by pest and weather; (some estimates put such loss to as high as a third of all food grain production in India). Often even the covered capacity is not actually available because old stock is lying in it and has not been cleared or disposed. The other problem is of distribution of this capacity. Many high producing states like Punjab face actual shortage frequently, even though 60% of all storage is in the north. The government has involved the private sector in building storage capacities. Companies like Adani Group, Kalpataru Group and newer companies like Star Agri-warehousing have come up to address this need. As of the end of 2018, a total of sixteen million tonnes of storage capacity has been tendered to private players to build and almost fourteen million tonnes has been completed and handed over as well. So, this is going to help and is an important aspect of the food chain to watch. This however is not without challenges. Speaking to several such private players, the commercial terms of the contracts have not been very favourable, and many private players are focusing more on building this infrastructure to lend out to private buyers rather than lease it to the government.

So, while the overall capacity is growing, its quality and distribution are improving slowly and is going to remain to be a challenge for the government to really step up on its MSP procurement in any big way soon.

But the bigger issue is storage capacity for the farmer. Up until now, farmers mostly sell their produce at the farm gate (to small aggregators) or take it to the designated mandi. Very few even use the local informal storage facilities run by local warehouse owners. Most times they may not know about it. If they do, the quality of those warehouses again is very bad. Some of the private players who started building capacity to give on long-term contracts to FCI, started branching out to lease it to private buyers like end consumers, exporters or traders. As a step further, they have started offering it to farmers directly too. This is the real deal which needs to be addressed, because if a farmer does not have access to storage, he has no choice but to sell his produce at the prevailing spot price. Modern warehouses that are coming up could provide a vital link in the chain. As mentioned, most of these also mainly service the buyers of the produce and options that could have been opened to the farmer are very scarcely available.

A new modern warehouse can actually be of immense help to the farmer. Not only is it a safe place to store while he waits for a better price, they would also grade it in a lab and based on a warehouse receipt, the farmer could actually borrow from a bank against such stock, hence he would be able to free his working capital and not be under pressure to sell his produce soon, if market prices were abnormally low. This again could boost income of the farmer without the government using tactical MSP which is more expensive for the government because many times, the mandi prices are low for short periods of time and are also manipulated by the agents. With this option available to the farmer, it can offset such mala fide practices as well as help him tide over short-term price drops, (when all the produce hitting the market together, especially in a bumper harvest year)

I have visited several of these modern warehouses as well as the FCI godowns. The contrast is stark. The new infrastructure is very impressive in terms of quality of construction, well-lit clean spaces, with security and pest control to prevent rodents from coming in. Many of these warehouses have a bank official sitting at the warehouse and once the farmer deposits his stock, post-inspection and lab testing (also at the warehouse); based on the warehouse receipt, the farmer could get the financing pretty much on the spot.

The only problem is that most of them cater to the buyers

and not the sellers. But with better marketing and more awareness by the farmer, this is improving. Over the last five years one of the warehouse owner told us, the farmer usage of his total capacity had gone up from 5% to almost 20%. This again ties up with one of my strongest observations — which is information scarcity. Not many farmers know that they can store their produce at a reasonable cost and even get financing against it.

Solutions Galore

The government is making efforts in multiple directions to maximise the realisation of the farmer and reduce or even eliminate the spread the middleman takes away. Enhancing rural infrastructure to provide good storage options to farmers is one, locating more mandis near the producing areas is another, bringing in more crops under the support prices and even paying the farmer just the difference where the government cannot procure, or store is another idea. Lastly, an electronic national market is a great idea as well. Even if some of these ideas are implemented, they will go a long way in raising the farmer's income in a structural and sustainable way and incentivise him to stick to farming.

Section 4
The Changing Social Fabric of Education and Women Power

Trip four — November 2017
Uttar Pradesh — Saharanpur, Gangoh, Baghpat, Samalkha.

This has been the most complex trip I have done so far, with a group of eight investors all having very different areas of interest. So, we took the format one notch higher to split even the village walk into pre-decided structured tracks. We also introduced the house visit as an extension of the open house and village walk. This house visit was before the focus group discussions took place in each track. Up until then we were only splitting the town meetings into tracks. We started with an open house and then split the group into three sub-groups of three or four people each and they spent the next hour or two in their own track, after which we got together for some more common meetings and visits before we headed for lunch and to town for further retail meetings. By this time, the science of planning such trips had turned into an art!

Trip Diary #9 — A for Apple

As part of our regular village visits, we took the group to show them a village government school. It was a primary school for pupils up to eighth grade and was a co-ed school with both boys and girls. While we were wrapping-up the last few interactions and discussions and moving towards the gate, one of our guests noticed a small section of the school which had kindergarten kids and was very keen to meet them. I did not have the heart to say no and walked over with him. There were about twenty kids in the classroom. The teacher was very excited to see visitors to her class and wanted to show case their understanding. One five to six-year-old boy got up and very confidently walked up to the blackboard and started writing alphabets in Hindi and spelling out the basics. We asked the teacher whether the children also knew English, and immediately another student got up and started writing A for Apple, B for Ball etc.... it was truly surprising that kids of such a young age were able to spell. While we turned back with a very interesting feeling in our hearts, my guest remarked that even his five-year-old in Hong Kong is not able to spell so well...

CHAPTER 9
Education Is as Good as the Weakest Teacher or Parent

The Steep Slope of Development and the Next Sixty Kilometres

Before I talk about what changes we are seeing on the ground on the education front, I would like to highlight the overall social infrastructure development. This one is worth drawing a chart on! But since I have promised myself to keep this book very reader-friendly I will just talk about it although somethings are just best depicted pictorially. One of the most startling truths about the rural economy is how narrowly spread progress is, and how stark the failure of the trickledown effect is. This has hit me several times during the initial trips to the extent that it was critical to design the trips in a way that we get to see the real picture by going deeper into the countryside. Our first few trips were around a sixty- to eighty-kilometre radius of a large city and we saw a very progressive, prosperous, rural economy. All households having two- and four-wheelers, all children with a college degree and using their own two-wheeler to go to the nearest town for white collar jobs. Progress Nirvana. After a few such visits we realised that this could not be representative, and we should insist on going deeper into the countryside. So, we started looking at villages and small towns at a hundred to a hundred and twenty-kilometre radius, and the experience was eye opening. The prosperity levels dropped like a cliff. We went from 1000-1200 household villages to 300-600 household villages and social infrastructure as well as income levels dropped dramatically. The impact of proximity to a big bustling city was disproportionate. That is why I call it the steep slope (downward) of development. Prosperity struggled to reach the next sixty kilometres and this observation has been made umpteen times at every visit. In fact, our trips evolved to a stage which each trip would have a visit to three kinds of villages. One at sixty to eighty-kilometre distance, the second at one hundred to one hundred and twenty kilometre distance and the third at around one hundred and fifty to one hundred and seventy-five kilometre distance. There was another way of measuring this — the census rank. Out of about six hundred thousand villages in India we would visit one in the top five thousand, another in the top fifty thousand to one hundred thousand ranking and one in the two hundred thousand to three hundred thousand ranking. This really started giving us the true flavour and contrast that existed in reality. It is hence that I was the least bit surprised when a friend mentioned a story about his local barber who just lived seventeen kilometres away from a large town like Mathura and recently requested him to sell him his second-hand TV. When my friend asked him why he needed a TV, he said his village is about to get electricity! Indeed, progress has been slow not covering sixteen kilometres in the last sixteen years of relatively high

GDP growth.

It is true that the future of any system depends on some core changes in the fabric or basic elements of society that can drive change. Education is one such major foundation on which much of the economy will have to be built. Access to cheap, good quality education with good infrastructure and willing parents is key. On the other hand, as more women get educated and join the work force, they are taking the lead in driving change and bringing more progressive behaviour and optimism to the ambitions of the villagers. This was one of the highlights of the various trips and a delight to think and read about...

The Education Reality

Education is the clear backbone of any economy's future growth, and India needs this change too. Hence an important part of rural assessment is always about what's going on in its schools. Hence almost on every trip, a stop at a local school was a must, and I am glad we incorporated it although initially we felt it should be treated as a non-core and optional sort of a stop. We had also always brought up this topic during our open house sessions addressed to the rural families. Several discussions with school principals, teachers, parents and students themselves bring out the status of education in rural India and what challenges are faced by them. There are four main observations that I would like to highlight here about education in rural India.

Firstly, that one of the most heartening observations across the visits has been that the educational basic infrastructure has been quite decent across villages of various income groups. Whether we visited a small village in Tamil Nadu or a mid-sized village in Rajasthan and even a large prosperous village in Haryana, it was really very interesting to note how each of the villages has a very large concrete structure of a school building and campus with proper boundary walls. It includes large play areas, cooking area, toilets and ample classrooms. The buildings look very well kept and maintained in terms of structure, painting and even the day to day cleaning. The classrooms are well appointed and fairly well-lit with large windows; so definitely a very decent, basic infrastructure. Outside every school is statutory statistical data which highlights the number of schools in the area, what is the enrolment, teacher strength, government grant utilisation etc., and that data is pretty much well-updated and fresh. Clearly this is what greets you when you enter, and it gives you a pretty positive feel. Sometimes teachers and the principal have highlighted the lack of computers for their lab but that would be the next step. The next thing that hits you when you enter these schools is the staff.

Secondly, that the staff at these schools, whether it is the teachers, the principal himself or even the administrative staff are extremely motivated and passionate about what they are doing. Most of them have been doing this for at least a decade if not more and clearly, they are not doing it only for the compensation—which is quite minimal. The enthusiasm is infectious and I believe every one of us left the school premises thinking what more we could personally do to help this cause. They are such evangelists. I vividly remember one long discussion with a principal who had been with the school for some eighteen years and he would not let us leave till we saw some of his recently acquired infrastructure (computers) and without meeting up with some of his students. He wanted us to see how well they can converse with us and how confident and clear they were about their careers. The pride that was overflowing was tangible and I really had to request people to move on to the next meeting as all my guests were so affected and impressed with his passion and updates. Even the teachers spoke so animatedly, the passion was visible and the best part was that they were not complaining or highlighting the negatives but just wanted to show us around their school and classrooms. There was so much positivity in them. It has always struck me how someone can be so motivated and passionate about things when the compensation is hardly anything to talk about. It must come from within. I think this is one of the nation's biggest strengths and assets — people working passionately in the social sector, and one should make every effort to not lose this.

Thirdly—and the most moving part—the ambitions of the school going children. This latter part where the kids want to become doctors, teachers or join the army, nicely links to the next chapter; that of the future of farm demographics and what impact is likely on the farm economics of this growing trend.

Fourthly, that parents' interest in educating their children has gone up manifold. Whenever asked what they would do with some extra income in hand, the quick response is always — spend more on children's education. This may not be visible everywhere all the time, but as a general trend it has been very clear that spending on education is the top priority of villagers everywhere. We did see some differences in some very low-income villages where the men in the house would not be very keen but even there the women were very clear that the children had to go to school. It has been a known thing that in India, a child is seen as an extra farm hand and hence a productive member of the family from very early on. Hence this change in attitude is something to take note off.

It is somewhat useful to measure the effectiveness of the education push which can be measured by how many students attend, how many teachers are there, with what qualifications, and how good is the curriculum and the tools available to teach including the basic infrastructure. This admittedly is quite mixed.

Number of students: Across the spectrum of villages visited over the last eight to ten years, the classrooms are not usually very heavily filled. Six to eight students in a class is what I have noticed most of the time. Clearly this teacher student ratio is not an intended one; and points to low participation. There are multiple forces at play here to understand this fairly complex topic. During the last few years, the student enrolments has gone through waves. There was a phase when they were dropping because parents did not see the value in it, as either teachers were few, books were not available, or parents felt kids were not learning much. Also, private schools have mushroomed all around the villages and word of mouth has highlighted the much better impact of sending them there. As I mentioned above, parents have been willing to spend on education, so they have sent their children to private schools even if they have to pay around three to four hundred rupees a month versus free education at the government schools. Recently however, enrolments have started going up again as there has been an improvement in teacher quantity and quality, as well a very big contribution from the mid-day meals as well as free uniforms. This is something only available in a government school and it is sad but good at the same time that a household sees so much value in one square meal for their child that it is enough motivation to send them to school. At times we have seen children even below the age of five being sent with their siblings to the school just for the food. Recently even initiatives like giving free bicycles for the children to commute to the school have helped boost the participation.

Number of teachers: Although we have not seen this first-hand very often, there are times and areas where teacher vacancies are not filled for months or even years. Due to not very attractive salaries it's not as if there are many qualified people applying for such jobs. Moreover at least a few times a year when there are local elections going on or the government is running some campaigns; these teachers get roped in to work full-time on those campaigns. Given a very multi-layered governance structure one can imagine that there is some or other such thing going on every three to six months. This is one of the biggest reasons why teachers are not able to attend school or even if they do attend, they are not able to pay full attention (particularly for checking test papers etc.). As per some reports there are some nine million government jobs lying vacant and in pursuit of less government and more governance, the government has justified such vacancies. A pertinent point here is that actually many states may be hiring adequate numbers of teachers but the rural and urban mix of how they are posted gets skewed due to various official and unofficial reasons. Some states hence will see less of a teacher supply problem than others. That brings me to the very closely connected next topic of teacher training.

Teacher training: The lofty ambition of uplifting the masses socially can only be fulfilled via strong building blocks which is well-trained teachers who will train the coming generation. As a child of a career teacher I will vouch for this more than anyone else. A student is only as good as his teacher. All the hard infrastructure and computers and mid-day meals will not do what a well-trained, motivated teacher can do. In most of our interactions, the teachers have complained that they would like to get training regularly on newer ways of teaching as well as on subject matter updates. This not only upskills them but also keeps the motivation going and may not cost too much. It would be a wise investment by the government to have a rotational, short training programme which teachers can be nominated to every six to twelve months based on their performance. This will incentivise them too. While it is important to train and motivate existing teachers regularly, it is equally important to establish a good supply funnel of well-trained and properly qualified teachers.

Curriculum: As an aside to our various rural trips, we always also rounded them up with meetings in Delhi or Mumbai with relevant experts or bureaucrats to get a fully rounded picture of the facts. One such interaction was with the then chief secretary of the Ministry of Education. We learnt here how the curriculum across the country has been linked to various state education boards and hence quality has been patchy. One big effort over the recent few years has been to get all government schools to only run NCERT (National Council of Educational Research and Training) curriculum and certified books. One of the complaints of parents has been that the rigour of the curriculum has been very low and hence progress on this front will have a very disproportionate impact if it starts encouraging more parents to send their children to the school. However, as education is on the concurrent list and hence also a state subject, the final call to implement curriculum changes is in the hands of the state. There have been some positive changes even with respect to the availability and distribution of NCERT books to various schools.

Tools and infrastructure: Some teachers and administrators have also pointed out that they need tools to make learning more interesting and fun. Whether it is educational toys for lower-level classes or computers for the higher-level ones. These are small investments with high returns. In fact, sometimes faced with lack of funding, school administrations have independently sought out donations from locals and other well-wishers to augment their resources to purchase some such apparatus. During few such visits, my guests have almost opened their wallets and shelled out some money.

There are three more important aspects worth noting.

Where Are the Boys?

During most of our visits while we were walking or driving around the village areas, we have often seen large groups of students walking to or back from school, wearing neat uniforms and carrying reasonably heavy backpacks and busy in routine banter. After some time, I started asking my guests if it was me or was it indeed that all the student groups we had spotted were girls. This made all of us more sensitive to this and we kept taking a more serious note of this pattern, and it certainly was the case. There were no boys to be seen. "Where were the boys?" we asked, and some responses we got pointed to the same old custom of using the male child as a farm hand.

But it was also to do with the fact that the girl child was much more sincere and keen to study and attend school more diligently. It is very encouraging and interesting to note how girls outnumber boys in the classrooms too. Nearly two-thirds of students enrolled are girls. The *beti padhao* (educate the girl child) scheme seems to have worked and is a visible trend over the last five to six years, although it may also be that girls move in larger groups and are more noticeable.

When I Grow Up. Double-Edged Sword?

It is good to send children of rural families to schools and get them a good primary education, but it is equally important to follow through by understanding what that is going to lead to, in terms of how education will change the ambitions of students and how they look at their careers. We have quizzed several students, male and female on their choice of future careers and the responses are spread across medicine, academics and the defence forces primarily, other than some saying they want to get a government job or work for the private sector. This is very encouraging and positive. Parents are ready to spend and give wings to their children so that they get a better life then the parents but this is a double-edged sword, and a very important question to ask. What happens to the farm economy if the youth is getting educated and abandoning farming and related professions altogether? This opens up the whole discussion about the future of rural demographics. This is taken up in detail in the next section.

Let's Get IT (I) Right! The Case for Vocational Training

But before that, there is another related topic to talk about and that is vocational training, for not only the rural folk but all youth in general. The government through the Ministry of Skill, Development and Training has a well-established scheme for this, called the ITIs (Industrial training institutes). These institutes run some hundred and thirty courses post-secondary schooling, for a six-month to two-year duration and teach things like garment production, electric and electronic appliance repair, and how to become a carpenter, plumber, electrician, mechanic etc. We visited a few of these institutes as well during our trips as the conversation decisively shifted towards jobs and employment opportunities to boost incomes of the rural folk. Again, the enthusiasm and commitment seen by the head and senior staff was palpable. They insisted for us to stay back and visit all the classes and talk to students etc. The admission to these is purely on merit but the number, capacity and proximity of such institutes is lacking and can barely impact a very small segment of the youth. The reason I bring this discussion in is that if there can be good courses and training to teach students higher end, more value-added work within the agriculture industry (dairy, mechanisation and high yielding techniques), we could retain more talent and skills within the sector and it could lead to the next generation taking their family farming business to new heights, rather than abandoning it all together.

Trip Diary #10: Career Woman

Another trip, another village, another *aanganwadi* (baby care) centre. For this one there were close to twenty of us. People from all over the world: Hong Kong, Singapore and America. After going through the routine questions and walk through of one of the larger nursery care centres, we were about to leave when one of the senior teachers requested us to wait and before we could say no she had called her daughter on the mobile and asked her to join us at the school. Seeing the enthusiasm in the mother's eyes we could not say no. Within minutes, a young lady in her mid-teens walked in very confidently and greeted all of us. Her confidence was impressive as we were an all-male crowd from overseas and it was commendable on the part of the mother to ask her daughter to come and greet so many strangers, that too men. It was even more impressive to see the young lady so confident and responding to our questions so calmly. It just needed a little prompting and off she went explaining to us that she did her primary education in a government school, moved to a private school for middle and higher secondary and now wants to go to a nearby town for her college. We asked her what she would like to do for her career, and pat came the answer — be a teacher like her mother! It was indeed very touching to see her enthusiasm in choosing a noble career and giving back to society, inspired by her mother!

CHAPTER 10
Women's Lib Is Taking Place in Indian Villages

Women power is growing in the villages. Whether it is more female students, more female teachers, *aanganwadis* manned by them or the multitude of Self-Help Groups (SHGs) that are improving the economic status of the women folk. A great trend to understand and enable further so that these women folk can become the key agent of change to drive growth. This also has other repercussions in terms of social dynamics. As these women get more powerful, assertive and in the driver's seat, they will drive spending and investing decisions too and hence marketeers will have to take note. As womenfolk come into the work force, (India has one of the lowest rates of women participation in the labour force), this itself can be an engine of growth. But more importantly than that, the male dominated village ecosystem that we have watched in countless Indian movies is about to change dramatically. It is very interesting to note here that in almost all the villages I visited, the village chief was actually a woman—although guided by her husband, she is already becoming the face of rural empowerment.

It is heartening to see how there is almost a two-speed social progress track in the villages. Despite being kept at home and asked to focus on household work, uneducated women folk are at the helm of social progress and are taking the lead in bringing change in their lives. Whether it's sending their sons and daughters to school, working in the day care centres as *aanganwadis* or becoming a part of the SHGs and creating some productive activities, it is indeed very visible during visits and is changing the fabric of our rural narrative. There are a few key aspects of this newly emerging social order.

More student enrolment: We spoke about the fact that more enrolments are slowly visible. But what is important to understand is what role the woman is playing in this and who is actually driving this. In many villages we have seen that the man of the house is either genuinely busy in the farm, seeking some NREGA work outside the home or is wasting away his time in unproductive pursuits, to put it mildly; and it is the woman of the house who is pushing for children to go to school or upgrade from local to private schools. She is the one saving the money or prioritising spend on incremental income to ensure they have enough to afford a proper education for the children. My foreign guests had come with some perceptions that village women keep their heads fully covered, do not come out to meet strangers and will never ever speak in front of their husband. They were pleasantly surprised to see these women being so vocal about their views and assertive in nature. It was eye-opening for them but admittedly for me too. Were the movies all depicting this wrongly or had things really begun to change? I would believe the latter.

Aanganwadis: The word means a courtyard house. The

148

government has a scheme whereby they run small childcare centres so that the parents can go back to work in the farms and kids can also get some early education before they actually start school, as well as something to prevent child hunger and malnutrition among infants. This was started in 1975. These centres also act as health support centres where infants can be given vaccines. Family planning advice and supply of contraceptives as well as education to mothers on child nutrition is imparted here.

These *aanganwadis* are manned by one or two women volunteers; volunteers because they really get paid a token amount—about fifty dollars a month for the worker and half of that for the helper, and it's clearly in their mind something they are doing for reasons other than money. We had the opportunity to meet several such women and each time it was a very encouraging experience. Their optimism and enthusiasm were palpable. Their pride in the work they were doing was really impressive. One of their other motivations to join this was so that they can be busy and meeting with people rather than wasting their time at home, and also as an escape from the daily routine.

SHGs and micro finance: India has seen a micro finance revolution during the last ten to fifteen years. The government of India through its various rural and cooperative bank branches has rolled out the schemes of SHGs which runs a joint, group liability-based lending programme for women who want to take small loans to start a business or cottage industry at home. These are really small activities like buying a sewing machine to start a small stitching service for the neighbourhood etc. Before I went on these trips, I would never have imagined that this concept was so popular in almost all the villages I went to. There is merit in the scheme because the bank matches the amount raised by the group of women because the group takes a joint liability of the borrower. I am not going to critique the pros and cons of such micro finance formats as that is not the objective here. I only want to highlight how women folk have embraced this in large numbers and how it reflects their progressive spirit and desire to break out of just tending to the kitchen and the kids. Most women of such SHGs that we met were again very positive and full of energy and that is what was notable. One stray case of a harrowed woman should not take away the overall buoyancy that one notices.

The village *mukhia*! This was really the icing on the cake. Almost all village chiefs I met, were women. They were wives of the *sarpanch* who had finished his first term and made his wife the chief for the second term, as law did not allow him to stand for a second term. Whatever maybe the reason, in our meetings the lady would come and listen to our questions and try to answer some of them while her husband helped out with the others. All such women *sarpanch* would not take their job lightly and it's only a matter of time that one takes it really seriously and actually takes the real governance into her hands. In fact, there were several lady chiefs who were actually de facto heads and not only in name.

With all this I wonder often that the males in the villages are just losing it and will just focus on playing cards on the roadside or drinking and gambling while the women folk really drive things forward...

Changing Social Infrastructure

Apart from these two fundamental changes taking place in rural India over the last decade or so, there have been a few other very important changes involving social infrastructure which have taken place relatively recently but with big impact. Something even Bollywood movies have been made about! Four main areas of development stand out: electricity, cooking gas, toilets and pucca houses. In my recent visits we took pains to make sure we got to see the reality on the ground and what impact it was having on the quality of life of the rural folk.

Electricity: One may wonder why a basic thing like electricity is something that needs highlighting here, but the truth is, as mentioned above even after sixteen to seventeen years of high growth, there were village just seventeen kilometres away from large towns that did not have electricity until a few months ago; and this story is often repeated across the country. Households finally have electricity and can have a normal light bulb and fan in the house as the very minimum. As incomes progresses, people have purchased a television, coolers or even some cooking or washing appliances. Initially this electric supply was not metered. Even now most of it is not. So, the household pays a lump sum of five hundred rupees a month based on how many connections they have coming in. So low usage houses are subsidising the high usage ones. Soon the metering is going to be rolled out as per one official we met in the village and that will have some impact on affordability and usage. On the other hand, it will be great for the local electricity supplier as they can bill higher and improve their long-suffering finances. In fact, recent advertisements in the paper are proclaiming how the government has just achieved full electrification of the country.

Cooking Gas: Another major change has been supplying the rural household with an LPG gas connection for home cooking. Up until now, the housewife had no such option and was forced to cook on open wood fires. This was very time consuming and also a health hazard due to the smoke that the lady had to inhale. With the LPG connection the women can cook the same food in less than half the time and be free to do other income generating activity as well as maintain good health. It has indeed been a boon, although women still use a mix of the gas and the wood fires depending on the weather (in winters the wood fire acts as a heater for the whole house) and urgency (if in hurry they would use the gas). This keeps the cost of gas down too.

Toilets: Even worse than not having electricity supply, most village homes did not have bathrooms due to superstition mainly as well as the cost angle. With the government grant and a lot of propaganda, lot of villages have seen toilets built in homes as well as in public places. This has again increased hygiene and privacy, especially for the women folk. We still hear that even after taking the grant from the government, less than half the funds have been used to make toilets and only half of those built are being used as toilets. No one can expect a hundred percent success rate, but a great start has been made. Many villages we visited had directly benefited from this and considered this the major positive achievement of the current government.

Pucca houses: A very large portion of rural housing is not made of concrete (cement and bricks) but made of mud and thatched roofs. The government has initiated a drive to convert all such *kuchha* houses to *pucca*. The government has a standard, template floor plan for each such house and gives the grant to the farmer in stages as the construction work progresses. During one of my visits to Madhya Pradesh, a farmer was elated that many of his friends and neighbours have got their houses and he was in queue to get his very soon. This initiative has also created jobs at the local level for civil contractors and masons as well as boosted demand for commodities like cement and other basic building materials like sanitary ware, paints, electric wiring etc.

All of this above together has laid the foundation for a stronger rural social infrastructure and quality of life as well as feelings of prosperity and good health. Education, women empowerment, housing, toilets, electricity and cooking gas have generally energised the villagers and filled them with more optimism and hope in general despite their constant struggle with core income from farming.

Section 5
Future of the Farm —
Demographics and Technology

The fifth trip: Madhya Pradesh – Rangwasa, Rau, outskirts of Indore

Moving into the farm. This trip was done in May 2018 in Madhya Pradesh on the outskirts of Indore and included villages like Rangwasa and Rau; and we refined one important aspect. We decided to start the trip — where else? — at an actual farm. We used to do regular farm visits with the farmer after the open house or the village walk, but I thought it would be more productive to actually conduct a detailed meeting at a farm where we all get to see the size, the crop, the irrigation systems and understand first hand from the farmer his cultivation and marketing process. Post this we start the open house which gets sharper post the farm visit!

Trip Diary #11 — Accountants and Factory Workers

It was a late May late morning and we had driven straight into the fields to meet one of the largest farmers in that area at his farm. We were dreading a very hot start to the day but were pleasantly surprised by large, shady banyan trees with leaves and branches swaying strongly under the lovely breeze that was blowing. After all, our worries were put to rest and this was a perfect start to this rural trip.

The farmer was old with grown-up sons and extended family of brothers living with him, as is common in rural India. His two grown-up sons were standing in the crowd as we sat down to have a chat. One of the topics that came up was shortage of farm hands and the fact that his kids have to help him during busy season. But did he not just tell me that one of his sons was an accountant and the other was a factory worker? Yes indeed. Both his sons had no interest to continue the farming legacy of the family and had qualified and moved out. It is only recently that due to bad employment conditions, they had returned to the village and hence were able to give a helping hand...

CHAPTER 11
The Future of the Farm — Impact of Changing Demographics

Thoughts for the Future

There are two main topics to focus on when we speak about the future of the farm. The first is about whether the farm economy will survive in the shape and form it is today given the demographic changes, i.e. will future generations even want to be engaged in farming, and if not, what happens? As demographics change and the younger generation has to take over the farms, it is not a given that they will. In fact, all signs point to the opposite, either because they are educated and have higher ambitions or because their holdings have dwindled to a size where they do not need to be fully occupied in the farm and earnings power is very low. Will the vacuum be filled by corporate entities or a reverse drain of urban folk coming to rural India? The second part, which is sort of connected, given fewer numbers of farm hands, is use of technology in farming; not just mechanisation but information and infra sharing as well. How future technology trends are or can be adopted in the farms, and more importantly will they?

There are several areas where new technology can be deployed but may need government support and push but also the right people on the farms to want to do it. We had the chance to dwell into both these issues and their sub-parts so it is worth spending some time on this topic.

Too Many Farmers?

The fact that the younger generation wants to leave farming, or the villages may not be such a bad thing in itself. I have often wondered and now there is an increasing school of thought among private economists and policy think-tanks too that indeed India may have too many farmers. Whatever schemes the government may launch to support their income, however many farm loan waivers they may give and whatever support prices they may announce, the fact that the denominator is too large is not going to change; and my guess is it will eventually not work. India has some one hundred and fifty million farmers who directly own land and use it for farming. This number has to reduce. On the flip side, the big shift from villages to cities that China experienced is being followed by a quick reversal and is not a path India needs to follow, but before jumping on to this aspect, it is worth understanding the reason behind the grain drain, as I call it.

The Big Indian Grain Drain

The grain drain has two causes. One is the fact that agriculture has become less profitable and involves more hardship which the younger generation is not willing to do. So even the second generation which is in their mid to late '30s is looking for jobs outside the farm. The second reason is the even younger, third generation who are leaving because they want to pursue a totally different career path of being a doctor, army, teacher, join the service economy or start a small business, and this trend is only going to grow as awareness increases and information is disseminated far and wide. We have to look at both of these causes separately as their solutions are also different.

Firstly, dropping profitability: Over the years, farmland parcels have been dropping in size. This is because as younger generations come into the family and they go their separate ways, the family land keeps getting divided and sub-divided between the sons, to a level that even a family owning twenty acres four or five decades ago, would now have seven or eight grandchildren owning just three or four acres each. As per basic economies of scale, such small parcels are not very viable as the usage of modern techniques is less possible and hence the cost to yield dynamics renders them very sub-optimal.

Hence, given already shrinking land parcels which has rendered farming unviable, even the larger farmers are facing a "grain drain", where the younger generation is not interested in taking up farming. They would rather join a factory, government job, run their fleet of taxis or even join the army if not becoming a teacher or a doctor. So, the first step is to make the core activity of farming lucrative as a business on a stand-alone basis, in such a way that at least the second or third generation of large farming families are not leaving the activity. For example, in countries like France or Netherlands, farming activity is still seen as a very lucrative "business" and not an activity of subsistence. To make the business inherently profitable and attractive, the trade has to be free of regulations.

The farmer should be free to produce what he wants and to sell it to whom he wants and at whatever best price the market can clear. We have dealt with this topic in section three on the supply chain and other bottlenecks in the value chain, so I will not dwell further into it.

More hardships: Moreover, given the low levels of mechanisation or irrigation, the dependence on the weather and on policy (support prices and mandi restrictions) the profession is seen as one with hardships; toiling in the farms with lot of physical labour involved and no guarantee of a good produce or price. It is soon going to become crucial for the government to put enabling systems in place for land aggregators or contract farming even if it is not corporates but cooperatives.

Secondly, although this topic of the generational shift in rural India and what it means for the farm economy has been touched upon widely in media and by columnists and rural economists and sociologists, it is more serious than that. That is what the multiple interactions have shown. The lack of interest in pursuing farming is so clear and widespread that it is literally a time bomb ticking and I don't say that to be alarmist. I don't think enough thought has gone into this and what it means. It is only a matter of another ten to fifteen years and this current younger generation (which is in primary school now) in their early teens gets to employment age. It will be apparent that they have no intention of joining the farm economy. By then the current second generation will be in their '60s.

So, the fact that the system just has ten to fifteen years to figure out a solution is quite scary actually. Who will man the farms? The issues to be sorted have all been mentioned in the chapters above; either allow contract farming in a proper way or make it more lucrative so that people don't leave the farms or new people enter in time. Even the incremental efforts by the government are in fact becoming self-fulfilling. Take for example more ITI-run vocational schools in rural India. This is empowering the youth with newer skills which allows them to pursue a non-agricultural career. Better quality school infrastructure, teachers and curriculum (NCERT etc.) is again pulling the youth away from agriculture. One suggestion could be to also encourage the rural youth and even actually urban youth to get skilled in agricultural skills and increase agricultural-related vocational courses and training opportunities. So even the landless can engage in agriculture-related activities and provide the much-needed manpower to the agricultural economy. Horticulture, floriculture, bee farming, animal husbandry and poultry farming do not necessarily need lots of land, unlike traditional farming.

The government should make parallel efforts to educate the rural youth to pursue non-agricultural careers but at the same time provide equal educational infra to train all youth (rural and non-rural) in agricultural skills to, in return get attracted by the agricultural economy which leads me to this new but promising trend.

And Its Reversal

The reverse flow: Urban folks are returning to their roots! It is ironic that while villagers try to move away from farming the stressed-out urban folk are actually seeking out ways to engage themselves in back-to-basics farming activities. Many young urbanites too are getting involved in things like organic farming. This trend should be explored more; how to help "rural start-ups" and create a reverse grain drain.

Trip Diary #12 — Technology

We walked inside the village and went up to one of the large homes with a big front porch. There were three wooden bed frames with rope work (*chaarpoy*) laid down for us and it was the venue for our focus group discussions on the use of high-speed internet in the villages. We had arranged for eight to ten men to come and meet us. Half of them had smart phones and half of those had just chosen the newest entrant into the Indian mobile service, due to initially its free pricing but stuck with it due to its much better coverage and much higher speed; to the extent that the other smart phone owners were planning to switch too, and the feature phone owners were looking to buy smartphones soon as well. So, we had a near 100% smartphone penetration in our midst.

We queried what they used this high-speed internet for. Cricket, You Tube and WhatsApp were the three main reasons. Very few said they check agricultural commodity prices or the weather, but one thing was clear that they all were pretty savvy in terms of knowing how to get the information they needed from the net, which is a great positive as the content providers, including the government, just need to push out the information; the pipes and the users are ready

CHAPTER 12
Technology and Its Rural Implications

A detailed discussion on the rural sector will not be complete without some thoughts on how the future could pan out. By now it will be amply clear to the reader that the rural economy is challenged with a lot of issues and solutions will have to be multi-pronged and will need a heavy dose of technology usage in the mix. It is indeed good fortune that a lot of innovation is going on just when the country needs it. It requires some will, some funding and a lot of implementation skills. There are three main phases and areas of technology filtration into the villages. The first is electricity, followed by the internet. Once these physical building blocks are in place, information can flow through seamlessly. Based on that, then apps can be launched to transact and finally usher in the share economy into rural India too.

Let's first look at the basic internet connectivity and its implications. Smartphones are already pretty ubiquitous in the villages and its penetration is probably much more than people think or statistics tell. Our own visits and multiple focus group discussion show this amply. So decent speed internet is widely available now in most villages via the cellular networks. In addition, the government has made efforts to modernise villages on various fronts and providing villages with fixed broadband connectivity. The Digi Gaon initiative is about that. The idea was to lay an fibre-optic network across all villages and at least connect some of the basic infrastructure to the pipe, to have a common consumer service centre which can act as a hub to which a villager can come to browse the net and get some educational or health advice going forward. Connecting Schools and dispensaries would be the second phase. Many private businesses have also tried to build a business model on this where a villager can come and do his e-commerce activity at an outlet assisted by the centre managers. During our various visits we clearly saw that there were several villages which had operational CSCs (Computer Security Centre) as well as private sector operator hub-centres, but it was not something rolled out on a wide basis. The fibre-optic network, known as the BharatNet, also was visible in certain villages where the pits were being dug at the outskirts of the village and in due course would reach the village centres. The BharatNet initiative involves laying of some ten million kilometres of optic-fibre to reach all two hundred and fifty thousand-gram panchayats and connect two to five Wi-Fi hotspots to it terminating at each of the six hundred and fifty thousand villages. This OFC network will provide a 100 mbps speed. The government has used the universal service obligation fund (a charge levied by the department of telecommunications on all telephone service operators) to fund this. This was to be implemented in two phases, getting completed by early 2019 or end of 2019. The first phase covering one hundred thousand-gram panchayats was completed by December 2017. The total cost has been estimated at Rs420bn. The government is in fact contemplating increasing the scope of this programme to cover all rural households with internet connectively and not just the village.

The second aspect is that of information access. The technology deployment in the farm can be broadly divided into two parts, pre-harvesting and post harvesting. Within pre-harvesting which is to ensure good crop production and prevent damage from pests and bad weather, it is very interesting to note how much is going on in this field. Companies like Skymet are deploying drones to help banks finance cropping activities, so that lenders can mitigate risk and hence lend more. These drones are also very effective in assessing crop damage and hence very powerful to insurers who provide crop insurance. Such technology which allows accurate assessment of claims, will only bring premiums down and make farming a more efficient and vibrant economic activity. On the post-harvest side, while there are government driven initiatives or driven by some private sector companies to create the infrastructure, there are also very interesting businesses being launched by companies who are taking advantage of technology and information.

Something that was launched many years ago — the e-choupal by the ITC Group — was trying to use information flow to provide the farmer with price information so he could decide when to sell his produce at which market. Since June 2010, this initiative now is spread across more than six thousand such kiosks, covering thirty-five thousand villages over ten states and covers four million farmers growing a range of crops like soya bean and wheat. E-choupal's primary objective was to help the company procure agricultural produce like wheat, directly from the farmers which were very fragmented and to avoid the intermediaries who would not ensure proper quality to the buyer or price to the seller. Roughly every five kilometres a kiosk was installed (which consisted of a PC with internet connectivity at a *sanchalak's* home). We visited a few e-choupals over the years. They have worked for certain crops in certain states, but the initiative also faced issues with physical infrastructure like power and internet connectivity. Hence with further improvement in that, such benefits can only increase. There have also been entities like the NCDEX (National Stock Exchange Commodity Exchange) who have tried through mobile apps to get real time price and weather information to farmers as well.

The third aspect is where we have apps going one step further — connecting seller to buyer directly, and helping in transactions. Companies who were in the rural infrastructure creation, have branched out to provide these B2B (business to business) portals — where they provide the quality check, logistics and transportation and not only within India but across countries as well. There have been many technology-based platforms which have tried to achieve the food economy nirvana; that is to remove the middleman and get the food from farm to fork with minimum added costs, intermediaries which help in maximising yields for farmers. In China we have seen such start-ups already getting valued at multiple billion dollars. As a further step to this we have the shared economy which has kicked in as well. Sharing of farm equipment and tractors in an 'Uber-like' way is already happening via companies like Trringo and others.

Industry estimates peg the value of the rental farm equipment market at around Rs150bn at a 35% mechanisation level. Consultants like Accenture estimate total digital agriculture services market opportunity to be around $4.5bn by 2020 in India. Companies like Trringo — promoted by the Mahindra & Mahindra group (leading tractor maker) is one of such companies started in 2016, who are trying to bring technology and the shared economy to increase the availability of mechanisation to farmers in a cheap and hassle-free manner, by the use of technology. This can be quite powerful because the tractor penetration is low and so is affordability. Already on a very informal basis, tractor and equipment rental is very popular across villages. In fact, doing our visits we have met several such farmers who rent tractors for their farms and we have met several tractor owners who rent out their tractors to other farmers and operate a fleet of tractors. In fact, we have not even encountered one owner who has even a little structured fleet operation. They are all just owning one or a maximum of two tractors which are also extremely old – ten to fifteen years minimum and are rented out, with or without the driver. It is strange that although the average life of a tractor is considered to be about eight years, fleet operators we have met own ten to fifteen-year-old vehicles and say that it is very cheap and easy to repair tractors and there is no need to buy a new one! The farmer user has echoed the same views mostly, rather than saying that they want to upgrade but can't afford to. Most new tractor buying is either a first-time purchase or a second purchase rather than an upgrade.

Agritech has become a buzz word and lots of start-ups are finding funding from VC (Venture Capital) and PE (Private Equity) funds. Last but not the least, I just read an article recently about the first Farmbots being sold by a start-up. They have built three robots called Tom, Dick and Harry which do various farm work more efficiently and smartly using AI.

Understanding these two trends of changing demographics and technology and putting all the issues facing rural India into context would be helpful and important as the rural folk embrace their future with a lot of hope and energy.

It is fitting that this book should end with this chapter as all the problems, challenges and facts shared in the chapters above can have a very elegant and efficient solution through technology. Technology can be present across all parts of the value chain — pre-harvest and post. From choosing the right crop, to figuring out multi-cropping patterns; from helping farmers to reach wholesale and retail buyers directly and to using supply chain solutions, better price discovery and better cost management through shared resources etc., it is not just hopeful to say that in the next ten to fifteen years, even if policy measures are status quo, technology progress and adoption can cause wonders to the farmers' prosperity.

CONCLUSION

This entire book can be summed up in a few sentences. All the problems I have highlighted can be sustainably fixed and start a virtuous cycle by changing a few things. In fact, just three...

Firstly, facilitate the aggregation of land by other farmers or corporates. World class farming practices can and will then be deployed, increase yields and hence make the business very attractive. It will stop the "grain drain" from rural India into the cities, keep the next generation fully engaged at the family farm and decisively release the rest to seek full time careers in urban India rather than hiding behind "disguised unemployment" as they do currently.

Secondly, allow the farmer to sell directly to the end customer. This will increase significantly the profit the farmer makes from his produce. This will tackle also the risk of inflation by hiking prices and will also not put any burden on the fiscal to procure and store tons of farm produce.

Thirdly, government should only involve itself through insurance schemes, for crop failure or pest attacks and health insurance to prevent loss of savings. This safety net will drive consumption up and make it less cyclical.

One last thought — proper dissemination of information

and eligibility criteria of all existing schemes will increase the use of the several dozens of schemes that already exist without the government having to spend an extra dollar.

This will give an elegant, hands-free agricultural model with minimum government involvement and predictable earnings for the farmer and hence a more balanced growth for the economy and turn it from a half-trick, to a one-trick pony!

Bibliography

Sources used
1. Average land size globally
Various media articles

2. Multicropping concept
https://www.jagranjosh.com/general-knowledge/cropping-patterns-and-cropping-systems-in-india-1517395777-1
https://en.wikipedia.org/wiki/Multiple_cropping

3. Irrigation level in India, Global and Asia
Various media articles

4. Food grain production and actual rainfall (Dept. of agriculture, IMD)

5. List of MSP crops
Various media articles

6. Rythubandhu scheme of Telangana/ Kalia scheme of Orissa and PM Kisan of NDA
https://indianexpress.com/article/explained/kalia-how-odisha-new-scheme-supports-farm-community-with-payments-5540259/
https://en.wikipedia.org/wiki/Rythu_Bandhu_scheme

7. History of NREGA
various media articles

8. Percentage of rural indebtedness and need for emergency money/ KCC usage and statistics (NAFIS)
NABARD All India Rural
Financial Inclusion Survey 2016-17

9. ICRIER study on KCC and indebtedness. Working paper number 357, Ashok Gulati, Tirtha Chatterjee and Siraj Hussain
Supporting Indian Farmers:
Price Support or Direct Income/Investment Support?

10. APMC statistics and e-NAM facts
https://en.wikipedia.org/wiki/E-NAM
http://www.enam.gov.in/NAM/home/index.html
https://yourstory.com/2013/05/agri-logistics-in-india-challenges-and-emerging-solutions
http://www.academia.edu/9060669/Agriculture_Supply_Chain_Management_A_Scenario_In_India
http://www.arthapedia.in/index.php%3Ftitle%3DAgricultural_Produce_Market_Committee_(APMC)

11. ITC e-Choupal details
https://economictimes.indiatimes.com/industry/cons-products/fmcg/targetting-10-million-farmers-in-e-choupal-network-by-2022-itc/articleshow/60464769.cms
https://en.wikipedia.org/wiki/E-Choupal
https://www.itcportal.com/businesses/agri-business/e-choupal.aspx

12. FCI storage statistics
http://fci.gov.in/app2/webroot/upload/Storage/FAQ_PEG.pdf

13. Some facts on ITIs
https://en.wikipedia.org/wiki/Industrial_training_institute

14. DigiGaon and BharatNet
Various media articles in the Economic Times, Business Standard, Business Line, Mint etc.

15. Rental farm equipment market and digital rural services market Accenture report
https://www.accenture.com/in-en/_acnmedia/597E512993C24B218EBF43F999278A50.ashx